GLOBETROTTER™

GW01081388

Th

BANGKOK

SEAN SHEEHAN

NEW
HOLLAND

GLOBETROTTER™

First edition published in 2007
by New Holland Publishers (UK) Ltd
London • Cape Town • Sydney • Auckland

10 9 8 7 6 5 4 3 2

website: www.newhollandpublishers.com

Garfield House, 86 Edgware Road
London W2 2EA
United Kingdom

80 McKenzie Street
Cape Town 8001
South Africa

Unit 1, 66 Gibbes Street,
Chatswood, NSW 2067
Australia

218 Lake Road
Northcote, Auckland
New Zealand

Distributed in the USA by
The Globe Pequot Press, Connecticut

Publishing Manager: Thea Grobbelaar
DTP Cartographic Manager: Genené Hart
Editor: Alicha van Reenen
Designer: Nicole Bannister
Cartographer: Nicole Bannister
Picture Researcher: Shavonne Govender

Reproduction by Resolution (Cape Town)
Printed and bound by Times Offset (M) Sdn. Bhd.,
Malaysia.

Although every effort has been made to ensure
that this guide is up to date and current at time
of going to print, the Publisher accepts no
responsibility or liability for any loss, injury or
inconvenience incurred by readers or travellers
using this guide.

Photographic Credits:
Peter Adams/jonarnoldimages.com: page 78;
Jon Arnold/jonarnoldimages.com: pages 32,
37; **Walter Bibikow/jonarnoldimages.com:**
pages 9, 12, 61, 79; **Alan Copson/
jonarnoldimages.com:** pages 7, 16, 30, 43;
Anders Blomqvist: pages 21, 34, 40; **Tom
Cockrem:** pages 23, 26, 33, 38, 41, 44, 62;
Gerald Cubitt: pages 8, 10, 11, 14, 17, 18,
22, 35, 42, 49, 74, 81, 83; **International
Photobank/Adrian Baker:** cover;
International Photobank/Peter Baker: pages
13, 31, 63; **Jean D Martin:** pages 15, 25, 29,
72, 73; **Buddy Mays:** title page, page 28; **Neil
Setchfield:** page 48; **Danny Levy Sheehan:**
pages 6, 77; **Jeroen Snijders:** pages 19, 20,
24, 27, 36, 45, 46, 51, 54, 71, 84.

Front Cover: *View of Bangkok from the Royal
Grand Palace.*
Title Page: *A girl dressed in traditional Thai
clothing at Wat Arun.*

CONTENTS

MAKE THE MOST OF YOUR GUIDE

Reading these two pages will help you to get the most out of your guide and save you time when using it. Sites discussed in the text are cross-referenced with the cover maps – for example, the reference 'Map B–C3' refers to the Central Bangkok Map (Map B), column C, row 3. Use the Map Plan below to quickly locate the map you need.

MAP PLAN

Outside Back Cover   Outside Front Cover

Inside Front Cover   Inside Back Cover

THE BIGGER PICTURE

Key to Map Plan

A – Greater
      Bangkok
B – Central
      Bangkok
C – Patpong and
      Silom Road
D – Excursions
      Map

USING THIS BOOK

Key to Symbols

⊠	– address	ठ	– entry fee
☎	– telephone	❶	– restaurants nearby
₪	– fax	🚌	– bus transport
💻	– website	M	– nearest Metro station
↻	– e-mail address	🛥	– Chao Phraya Express Boat
⊕	– opening times	🚤	– nearest Skytrain station

Map Legend

motorway		main road	**Thanon Rama IV**
national road		other road	Thanon Sarasin
main road		mall	SAMPENG LANE
minor road		MRTA under-ground train	Silom
railway		BTS sky train	Siam
river	*Khlong Ong Ang*	built-up area	
dam		market	
ferry route	– – – –	building of interest	Royal Grand Palace
ferry pier	*Siriraj Pier* 🛥		
route number	9 3215	museum	
city	**BANGKOK**	bank	
major town	⊙ Ayutthaya	university	
town	O Hua Hin	college/school	
large village	◎ Pak Tho	shopping centre	Ⓢ *Central*
village	O Thung Luang	embassy	🏳 Dutch Embassy
airport	✈ ✈	library	📖
cave	*Khao Sam Muk* 🔴	post office	⊠
temple	▲ Wat Suthat	tourist information	i
golf course	⌐	place of worship	△
bathing beach	🏖		
diving	🤿	police station	●
hotel	Ⓗ VIENGTAI	bus terminus	🚍
place of interest	★ *Giant Swing*	hospital	⊕
park & garden	*Lumphini Park*		

Keep us Current

Travel information is apt to change, which is why we regularly update our guides. We'd be most grateful to receive feedback from you if you've noted something we should include in our updates. If you have any new information, please share it with us by writing to the Publishing Manager, Globetrotter, at the office nearest to you (addresses on the imprint page of this guide). The most significant contribution to each new edition will be rewarded with a free copy of the updated guide.

OVERVIEW

Above: *The Skytrain is the easiest way to see the city.*

A Biased City

The Chao Phraya glides in a curve through the city but the division it creates is an unequal one. Nearly all your time is likely to be spent on the east side and, with one notable exception, all the hotels are here and so too are the restaurants and nightlife. The west side of Bangkok is called Thonburi and crossing over to it can provide an instant therapy for urban blues. Thonburi boasts a superb hotel with excellent restaurants (*see* page 63), one major temple and a rural setting of surprising tranquility

---

BANGKOK

Very few cities of the world, some would say none at all, can equal Bangkok in terms of a total sensual experience. Exciting, exotic, daunting and overwhelming, sooner or later you will find the excess of it all too much, but this will not last if time is allowed for relaxation and rest.

Some six to nine million people (depending on how the city area is defined) are jostling for a place in this sprawling metropolis so it is natural to feel overwhelmed by it all. Fortunately the most engaging sights and attractions are in the centre of the city. When it is time to disengage and escape what can seem like organized chaos there are a number of short excursions that can be enjoyed before returning with your batteries recharged.

The key to getting the best out of your time in Bangkok is careful planning, especially with regard to modes of transport and the prioritizing of your interests. Too much shopping or too many temples will induce sensory overload so plan a range of activities and vary the rhythm of each day. There is a time for taking a taxi, a *tuk-tuk* or train but allow for some evening walks and daytime boat rides, even cycling (*see* page 48), and surprise yourself by eating and drinking in some of the entirely different places that can be nosed out with the help of this guide.

The Land

One long and life-giving river, the 352km Chao Phraya, flows from central Thailand to the coast and largely accounts for Bangkok's existence. It flows south, irrigating an extensive region of rice paddies, and for centuries the river has attracted human communities along its banks. At one time, Bangkok was situated at the mouth of the river as it emptied into the Gulf of Thailand, but over the millennia an expanse of sediment, still increasing, accumulated and separated the city from the coast, so that today there is little sense of Bangkok being near the seaside. The Chao Phraya River, on the other hand, remains a constant presence and is used daily by residents and savvy visitors who appreciate the time it saves in traversing the city and avoiding the constant traffic fumes. The city's amphibious origins are also evident in the network of canals, *khlongs*, that are still used and the best way to experience this is by way of a **Thonburi tour** (*see* page 21) or by taking a journey on the very useful canal that runs across the city.

Celebrating Water
The middle of April, when temperatures are at their highest, brings the **Thai New Year** and plenty of water – though not directly from the sky. Buddha images are bathed with respectful care but ordinary mortals are doused with exuberant excess and you can expect a bucketful over your head if in the Khao San Road area between **13** and **15 April**.

Climate

Temperatures remain high in the capital and rarely fall below 26°C (79°F). November to January are the coolest months and only in April and May is 30°C (86°F) reached; the rest of the year remains fairly constant at around 28°C–29°C (82–84°F). Rainfall is

Below: *The Chao Phraya River divides the city into two unequal halves; most of your time will be spent on the east side.*

What's in a Name?
The answer in the case of Bangkok is quite a mouthful of syllables, the official name being '*Krung Thep Mahanakhon Amon Rattanakosin Mahinthara Ayuthaya Mahadilok Phop Noppharat Ratchathani Burirom Udomratchaniwet Mahasathan Amon Piman Awatan Sathit Sakkathattiya Witsanukam Prasit*'. This is translated by Wikipedia as: 'The city of angels, the great city, the eternal jewel city, the impregnable city of God Indra, the grand capital of the world endowed with nine precious gems, the happy city, abounding in an enormous Royal Palace that resembles the heavenly abode where reigns the reincarnated god, a city given by Indra and built by Vishnukarn.'

more variable, with January and February very dry, averaging only 20mm (0.86 in) but then steadily increasing between May and September – meaning very heavy downpours and flooded roads – before tailing off towards the end of October. When heavy showers fall, some taxi drivers will not use their meters and consequently charge more.

History in Brief

The context for understanding the early history of Bangkok, and why it developed where it did, is a far wider region of South-East Asia than the present-day boundaries of the country. Territory that now constitutes the independent states of Laos, Vietnam, Cambodia and Burma, as well as Thailand, was fought over by a succession of rulers and ethnic groups. Beginning in the late 13th century, a Thai kingdom developed and came to base itself on the banks of the Chao Phraya, where a new city, Ayutthaya, was founded. This powerful Ayutthaya kingdom supplanted the older Sukhothai kingdom and over the following centuries came into conflict with Burma and Cambodia. Relations with Burmese rulers were especially fractious and in 1767 a decisive stage was reached when Ayutthaya fell to the Burmese after a seven-year siege. The city was laid to waste.

The loss of Ayutthaya forms the backdrop to the history of Bangkok because it was in the aftermath of the fall of the Ayutthaya kingdom that one of its provincial governors, a man called Taksin, emerged to challenge the invaders. He formed an army and was successful in expelling the Burmese, but realized that a more defendable base than Ayutthaya was desirable for future security. He choose to move some 90km (56 miles) down the Chao Phraya River to where a small trading centre by the sea had earlier been established, known as Bang Makok (the 'place of the olive plums').

Taksin based himself on the west side of the river and with the help of General Chakri set about re-establishing a Thai kingdom and conquering Laos. He was, however, deposed and executed by powerful interests and General Chakri was crowned King Rama I in 1782, the first ruler of the Chakri dynasty. The new king moved to the east side of the river, renaming it Krung Thep ('City of Angels'), but the old name continued to be used.

Rama I set about building a palace in Bangkok that would evoke the glorious era of Ayutthaya, and statues, stones and bricks from the old capital were brought downriver to adorn his new home. At this time, people lived close to the river or the many canals that threaded their way through the land. The canals also provided a defensive feature for the protection of the king and the palace complex was planned inside a ring of two canals, to which a third was added later. Benefiting from the sense of security this provided, Rama I was able to deal with the Burmese and also extend Thai sovereignty to include a number of Malay states to the south. Rama I is credited with establishing a strong sense of Thai cultural identity and making Bangkok the country's

Above: *A bearded sage at Wat Pho.*
Opposite: *Ruined temple at Ayutthaya.*

A Revered King

Thailand's fractured political history over the last fifty years, as well as destabilizing turns in the economy, has made the royal family an emblem of stability and rational order. King Bhumibol Adulyadej, the 9th king in the Chakri dynasty and so Rama IX, has been on the throne since 1946 and is treated with a degree of respect that cannot be matched by any other constitutional monarch. Criticism of the monarchy is an offence by law, and occasionally foreign visitors have found this out to their cost, so bear this in mind. When Rama IX dies he is expected to be succeeded by his oldest son, Crown Prince Maha Vajiralongkorn, but whether he will enjoy the esteem accorded to his father remains to be seen.

Above: *Gilded architecture at Wat Phra Kaew, the most revered of all Thai wats.*

permanent capital.

By the time of Rama II's rule (1809–24), European commercial interests were arriving in Bangkok but there was a steadfast refusal to grant them the kind of access they sought. Rama III (1824–51) continued to insist on Thai autonomy and so did his successor – although Rama IV (1851–68) successfully introduced Western technology to life in Bangkok. Rama IV set about reconstructing aspects of the city along European lines and under his direction the first roads were built.

A keen sense of nationalism kept imperial powers at bay for the first four decades of the 20th century but Thailand succumbed to foreign power when the Japanese arrived in Bangkok and a forced military alliance was made in 1941. After the end of World War II, as the Cold War was played out in Southeast Asia, foreign interests competed for influence in Thailand. Military coups and counter-coups became endemic and, by the time of the Vietnam War, anti-communist and pro-American interests had gained the upper hand.

Political struggles for power continued throughout the 1970s and '80s and Bangkok became the focus for demonstrations against military governments that periodically usurped civilian rule. In 1992 the largest demonstration of all took place in Bangkok, following a coup in 1991, and hundreds of protesters were killed and injured when the army opened fire.

Today constitutional rule has been re-

Protected by Indra

Bangkok's official seal depicts the god Indra, god of thunder, riding on the elephant-like, three-headed Erawan and brandishing a lightning bolt. The ability to inflict lightning is not, as with the Greek god Zeus, a symbol of power and wrath but an expression rather of the benign wish to banish drought and precipitate rain – essential for rice harvests.

stored, and Bangkok is now a peaceful and thriving metropolis. Material progress, however, has seen relentless modernization over the past few decades, but the process has been a haphazard and largely unplanned one and as a result a sprawling urban geography presents the visitor with an orientation headache. There is no obvious centre to the city and the layout of main roads is too complex to master in a short visit. This means that the location of your accommodation will have an enormous bearing on where you eat, shop and seek entertainment, so bear this in mind when planning your visit.

Government and Economy

Thailand has been a constitutional monarchy since 1932 and although the king's political power is minimal he exerts a tremendous influence and is deeply revered; you will see photographs of the royal family everywhere.

A new democratic constitution, drawn up in 1997 – the 16th since 1932 – got off to a shaky start due to a severe economic crisis, but it survived intact. Government is conducted by a parliament, elected by the people, and human rights and freedoms are guaranteed by law. Corruption remains rife, however, and election time in rural areas involves the widespread buying of votes. One politician, noted for his success in this respect, was dubbed 'the walking ATM' by journalists. The present government is led by a multi-millionaire, Thaksin Shinawatra, and critics are vociferous in their allegations of corruption in government administration.

The Buddha
Buddha, the 'enlightened one', is not a god, but the name given to Siddhartha Gautama, born in Nepal around the 6th century BCE. He renounced his privileged upbringing in favour of an ascetic lifestyle and left his home to travel and converse with people about the nature of existence and ways of living a good life. He attained spiritual enlightenment in middle age, after a long period of contemplation under a *bodhi* tree at Bodh Gaya in India, and entered a state of nirvana before dying at the age of 80. Nirvana, the state of perfect beatitude, brings an end to all desire and is typically represented by the figure of a reclining Buddha.

Below: *The National Parliament in Thailand's constitutional monarchy.*

The Way of the Buddha
The Buddha taught that life is suffering, brought on by desire, and the conquest of suffering is possible by uprooting desire and following an eightfold path – right view, right thought, right speech, right action, right livelihood, right effort, right mindfulness and right concentration – which translates as the traditional virtues of moderation and compassion and the avoidance of excess. The eightfold path is a guide to help one cope with the ever-changing flux of transient existence by focusing one's attention on the need to overcome desire and reach a state of detachment.

Opposite: *Saffron-clad Buddhist monk.*
Below: *Thai woman in eye-catching traditional dance dress.*

Bangkok is benefiting from a dynamic economy and international trade. The main exports are agricultural products, textiles and processed food and the robust economy is further strengthened by tourism.

The People

Thai people are thought to have originally hailed from southern Thailand, moving into what is now Thailand around the 10th century. In more recent centuries, Chinese people settled in parts of the country and established themselves as an economically important group of traders and merchants. Today, Thai-Chinese make up a sizeable proportion of Bangkok's population and are not just confined to the city's Chinatown. Unlike in most other states of Southeast Asia with a significant Chinese population, racial relations are harmonious.

Thailand's population well exceeds 60 million but while the average density is just over 120 per km^2 this catapults to over 3500 for Bangkok. The city is a magnet for impoverished people from rural areas and most of the workers you see on construction sites and in low-paid service industries are from outside the capital. The northeast of the country, known as Issan, is the poorest region and contributes a disproportionate percentage of Bangkok's poorly paid workers. Lao-speaking and Khmer people are concentrated in Issan and they too flock to the capital to find work. Ethnic Malays, making up some two million of the country's population, are present in the deep south of Thailand but not significantly in Bangkok. There is, though, a Thai-Indian presence in parts of the city and mosques are not uncommon, although you will hardly notice them given the plethora of Buddhist temples.

Buddhism is Thailand's state religion and the overwhelming majority of Thais are followers of the Theravada tradition. The religion spread from India – hence the incorporation of Hindu gods like Indra and Vishnu – and is now an integral part of Thai thinking. The doctrinal aspects of Buddhism are less important than the emphasis on right ways of living and the clocking-up of spiritual merits. Ideally, this means becoming a monk and so every Thai male is expected to spend some part of their life as a practising monk. Women can also become monks but this is not uncommon. For non-monks, merit-making – which increases the chances of being reborn as a better and happier person – is achieved by a variety of everyday practices. A short visit to a temple or shrine is one such measure and this helps explain why the Erawan shrine (see page 27) in the heart of the city is always being frequented by Thais who find the time in a busy daily schedule to pay their respects here.

The strong influence of Buddhism in Thai life is not overbearing or rigidly conformist. Sanuk, a key concept in Thai culture, translates as 'fun' and there is a light-hearted aspect to everyday life that makes one forget this is a country where 90% of the people follow the same religion. There is a deep-seated sense of respect for other people and loud or aggressive behaviour is frowned upon and regarded as boorish. The famous Thai smile is not the invention of a public relations company and really does express a sane and balanced approach to life.

Monks in Bangkok
You will certainly see monks when visiting a city temple or the Grand Palace but you will need to be up very early in the morning to witness the traditional start to the monk's day: the receiving of alms, in the form of food for breakfast, from citizens of the neighbourhood. If you arrive at Wat Benchamabophit (see page 36) before 07:00 monks can be seen on Nakhon Pathom, the street that runs parallel to Rama V Rd, receiving alms. A less ascetic side to monkhood is also observable on the streets of Bangkok and seeing a saffron-clad customer checking out the latest mobile phone in a shop is not a rare sight.

⊙ *See* Map B–A4   ★★★

CHAO PHRAYA RIVER

The mighty Chao Phraya River plays a vital role in the life of the city. Commercial barges transport heavy loads along it and every day thousands of city dwellers use the river to get to and from work. Visitors also use it as a handy way of avoiding long taxi or bus trips to reach key attractions. Apart from its practical advantages, the Chao Phraya is worth experiencing in its own right. Take one of the cross-river ferries or go at night, when the Express boats have stopped running, either from the terrace of the **Oriental** (*see* page 60) or by using the Peninsula's **free boat** to cross to the east side.

Although the boat service runs further downriver than Central Pier, also known as Tha Sathon, you can think of this pier as the starting point; it is designated as such by the boat company, with the piers upriver from it numbered as N1, N2 and so on.

Join one of the special tour boats that run as far as Banglamphu. A guide on board points out the major sites on both banks of the river and a concise guidebook helps make sense of the journey. The ticket lasts all day so you can disembark at any of the piers it uses and then re-join another tour boat later; the ticket is also valid for any of the non-tour boats.

Chao Phraya River
For cross-river trips, small boats run throughout the day from alongside the piers used by the Express Boat Company.
🚤 The Chao Phraya Express Boat Company
🕐 05:30–19:30 Mon–Fri; 05:30–19:00 Sat–Sun (the last boat of the day flies a blue flag)
💰 B6–25
Cross-river Ferries:
🕐 06:00–21:00.
💰 B2

Tours
Tours depart from Central Pier (Tha Sathorn), next to Saphan Taksin station
🕐 every half hour, between 09:30 and 15:00
💰 Tickets cost B75 at Central Pier
☎ 026 236 001, ext. 100, 106

Below: *Experience a journey on the Chao Phraya River.*

See Map A–C6 ★★★

CHATUCHAK WEEKEND MARKET

This is far more than a shopping destination and you need not come here with any intention to make a purchase – though it is difficult to leave without finding something. The sheer concentration of so much merchandise squeezed into so many stalls (somewhere in the region of 8000) is a phenomenon that will put to shame your local market back home. An early start for the train ride north to Chatuchak is worth the effort because by midday this vast market, spread out over 12ha (30 acres), is heaving with people and utter exhaustion will kick in at some stage. Maps of the market are available from the TAT office but you might wander off your intended route and become confused by the multitude of lanes, each one packed densely with stalls. The central clock tower is a useful marker if you do get lost or separated. **Nancy Chandler's Map of Bangkok** includes a detailed breakdown of the market, aimed squarely at the visitor, and is worth studying before you arrive. City residents come here for everyday items for the home and bargains like second-hand Levis while visitors tend to seek out the arts and crafts and knick-knacks. Sections 25 and 26 contain the bulk of craft items, like wood carvings, textiles and souvenirs, and sections 22–24 are good for clothes and accessories.

Although it seems chaotic, there is an order and etiquette to Chatuchak. Prices are not fixed, of course, and a degree of bargaining is essential but this is not like the market at Patpong (*see* page 24) and complete rip-offs are unlikely.

Above: *Chatuchak Weekend Market demands stamina, and is not for the fainthearted or the claustrophobic. Arrive early to enjoy stress-free shopping.*

Chatuchak Weekend Market
⊠ Kamphaeng Phet Rd and Phahon Yothin Rd
⌚ 08:00–18:00, Sat and Sun (sections 25 and 26 also open Fri 14:00–18:00)
🚇 Mo Chit (Exit N8)
M Chatuchak Park
🍴 Le Danang (*see* page 70)

Tourist Information:
⊠ TAT information office inside Gate 1 on Kamphaeng Phet 2, close to the metro station

 See Map B–A4 | ★★★

ROYAL GRAND PALACE

This is the royal heart of **Rattanakosin**, the area chosen for residence by **Rama I**. The Grand Palace still functions as a royal location for ceremonial events, although the king and his family now live in Dusit, and many of the buildings on the site are off-limits to visitors. There is a lot to see in this complex, the most visited site in Bangkok, and you will need the map that comes with your ticket in order to find your way around. Bring a camera if you have one, and a cap of some kind is useful for protection against the sun – for most of your visit you will be in the open and there is very little shade. A small pair of binoculars helps you appreciate the decorative artwork of the multi-tiered roofs and, as always, have a bottle of drinking water ready to hand.

The major temple is **Wat Phra Kaew** and Thai visitors come here to venerate the **Emerald Buddha**, a tiny image that is held in awe as an emblem of Thailand's spiritual identity. It was discovered in the 15th century inside a *chedi* (the tower of a temple where holy relics are kept) and ended up in Laos for some two centuries until brought to Bangkok by Rama I at the end of the 18th century.

The building shimmering in the sunshine outside the temple, **Dusit Maha Prasat**, is typical of the visual splendour of the Grand Palace. The roof is a work of art, set off by colourful tiles and flamboyant bird figures, and topped by a magnificent golden spire.

Prasat Phra Thep Bidorn, also called the Royal Pantheon due to its life-sized statues of Thai kings, is usually closed to the public

Royal Grand Palace
✉ Na Phra Lan Rd
☎ 026 235 499, or 022 220 092
🕐 08:30–15:30 daily
🚤 Tha Chang pier
🚌 To and from Siam Square: 8
♿ Admission: B250 (ticket includes entry to Vimanmek Palace, *see* page 32)
🍴 Keang Wang (*see* page 70)
Tours
English-language tours, free, from 10:00 onwards; 2-hr personal audioguide available for B100
Dress Code: Do not wear T-shirts, sleeveless vests, shorts or slip-on sandals. Shoes and some permissible garments are available for day use; free but ID or a deposit required and returned when leaving.
Warning: Beware of unscrupulous touts, well-dressed and kindly spoken, who tell you the Palace is closed for the day or the morning. They will suggest an alternative visit to some temple or other but this is a ruse for a shopping trip and their hoped-for commission.

ROYAL GRAND PALACE

See Map B–A4   ★★★

but the exterior is impressive. It displays features of **Khmer architecture**, like the row of eight *prangs* (the central towers of a Khmer temple) on the east side, and there is a scale model of the major Khmer temple in Cambodia, Angkor Wat.

Another building that is usually closed but still worth visiting is **Chakri Maha Prasat**. The story goes that some members of the royal family, alarmed at the liberties taken by the English architect who was commissioned to design the building in 1882, insisted on Thai-style spires being added in order to balance the structure's European appearance.

Not to be confused with Chakri Maha Prasat is the nearby **Dusit Maha Prasat**, designed as an audience hall for Rama I. You can walk inside to admire the delicate artwork using mother-of-pearl, though what will first catch your eye is the tiered roof and the ornamentation in the form of fabulous birds and the tails of water birds.

Also worth seeing are the **Ramayana Murals** decorating the walls of long arcades, carefully restored since they were first painted in the late 18th century. The narrative told in the pictures is a series of adventures, originating in Hindu India but which spread to Thailand; you would need a knowledgeable guide to explain the plots, but the meticulous artwork itself is a joy to behold.

The Royal Grand Palace
Situated on the banks of the Chao Phraya River, the Grand Palace occupies an area of over 1.5 km² and there is too much to take in on a single visit. King Rama I, when he moved his capital to Bangkok from Thonburi, wanted to replicate the architectural plan of the royal palace that had been destroyed in Ayutthaya. Building work began in 1782 and continued for many years, with new buildings being periodically added to the original plan.

Opposite: *A multitude of gilded figures adorn the Grand Palace.*
Below: *The temples, palaces, cloisters and museums of the Grand Palace.*

Jim Thompson's Museum
✉ Soi Kasem San 2, Rama 1 Rd
☎ 022 167 368
🕑 09:00–17:00 daily
🚇 National Stadium (Exit 1)
Canal Transport: Hua Chang pier
💰 B100 (under 25, B50)
Tours: Compulsory, every half hour or less
🍴 Café, bar, restaurant and shop
💻 www.jimthompson.com
Warning: As with the Grand Palace, touts are on the lookout for anyone they think could be convinced that the place is shut for the day. Ignore their suggestions of an alternative trip somewhere else.

Below: *Western influences are obvious in Jim Thompson's Museum.*

See Map B–F4   ★★★

JIM THOMPSON'S MUSEUM

Jim Thompson was an American who worked in Bangkok in intelligence during World War II and came back after 1945 to settle down in the city. It seems he single-handedly brought **Thai silk** to the attention of the West and by doing so was largely responsible for establishing its importance in the national economy. He wanted to live in a traditional Thai setting and had authentic teak houses in the vicinity of Bangkok dismantled and reconstructed in the heart of the city, close to an area where silk weavers lived and worked. These houses, filled with high-quality Thai artwork, are now open to the public and the compulsory tour focuses on the history, aspects of the architecture and the fine contents. Jim Thompson lived here for seven years but disappeared under mysterious circumstances in Malaysia in 1967 and, because his body was never found, a variety of lurid theories have been put forward – though the most prosaic explanation, that he was knocked down by a vehicle and the body hidden by the frightened driver, seems the most convincing.

As well as hearing about the mysterious disappearance of Jim Thompson, you will see on the tour some exceptional **Buddha images**, superb examples of cotton paintings, porcelain and handcrafted furniture collected over the years by Thompson to adorn his residence. (Photography, though, is not allowed.)

See Map B–B2 | ★★★

KHAO SAN ROAD

Khao San Road was once the preserve of impecunious backpackers seeking dirt-cheap accommodation and as such it gained a reputation as the best place in the city to meet fellow travellers, swap information and share quixotic

tales of life on the road. The area is still a magnet for young travellers but over the years quite a sophisticated infrastructure has developed for visitors and it now attracts a diverse crowd of sightseers. **Hotels** and **guesthouses** have sprung up catering for low to middle-range budgets and the range of places to eat is expanding all the time. Khao San Road itself is home to a bustling **street market**, specializing in clothes for the young, souvenirs, DVDs and CDs, plus an abundance of **cybercafés** with competitive Internet rates. Come evening time, Khao San Road and smaller streets and lanes running off it light up with bars and restaurants and a heady, very un-Thai atmosphere prevails.

At night, taxis congregate at the riverside end of Khao San Road and you will need one if not staying in the area because the Chao Phraya Express boats will have stopped running. To arrive in daylight, take a boat to **Tha Phra Athit Pier** and walk to the left once out on the street, and follow it as it bends to the right where, on the other side of the road near the river, there is a pleasant park. Following the bend of the road, turn right at the main crossroad into Chakrabongse Road

Above: *The quality of merchandise in Khao San Rd, a street market in its own right, is not high, but suitable for souvenirs and small gifts.*

Khao San Road
⊠ Khao San Rd, Banglamphu
🕓 08:00 to the early hours of the morning
🚤 Tha Phra Athit pier
🚌 To and from Siam Square: 30, 15, 47, 79 (on Thanon Ratchadamnoen Klang); to and from the Grand Palace: 53 (on the south side of Thanon Phra Athit.
🖥 www.khaosan road.com
Tourist Information: Bangkok Information Office, ⊠ Thanon Phra Athit (turn to the right on Thanon Phra Athit after exiting from boat pier), ☎ 022 576 124.

🌼 *See* Map B–A4 ★★★

Traversing the Khlongs
If you sit at the end of the bench seats then you risk the occasional light splash; sit in the middle and you have to clamber over other passengers when wishing to disembark. Either way, as the canal opens up views of what lies behind the glitzy steel-and-glass metropolis, you will see a side of Bangkok that is not always experienced by visitors. Keep a map close to hand, because the canal stops are not clearly marked, and count the stations to where you want to go.

Below: *Trips on the water offer a welcome relief from the hot and crowded city.*

and on the left, after about 250m (273yd), Khao San Road begins. If the crowds become too much, retrace your steps back to the boat pier because the park area you pass is close to Thammasat University and it is a far less noisy neighbourhood with quirky places to rest for a drink and a meal.

KHLONGS (CANALS)

Bangkok was chosen as the site for a new capital because of its defensive position on the river and at the time a series of canals provided the only means of getting around. Roads came much later – hence the city's old epithet Venice of the East – but the canals remain and they are still part of the city's transport infrastructure.

There are different ways to experience the *khlongs* of Bangkok. To explore the canals of **Thonburi**, across the river on the west side, there is a choice between guided tours and the rental, with a driver, of a long-tailed boat (so called because the

Khlongs (Canals)

☆ *See Map B–A4*   ★★★

diesel motor is attached to a projecting shaft that carries the propeller). For guided tours, you need to know exactly what the trip takes in because some of them make up the time by calling in at a snake farm or highly commercial floating markets while some take in a visit to **Wat Arun** (see page 14) or the **Royal Barges National Museum** (see page 25). The hire of a long-tailed boat, with a driver, can be negotiated from main piers such as Tha Chang (N9) or Tha Thien (N8); a trip at sunset can be most enjoyable.

For trips on the east side of the river, long-tailed boats operate like the Chao Phraya Express boats and stop at designated stations along the canals. The stations themselves are not always easy to find and it is advisable to stick to the much-used route between Tha Phanfa near **Democracy Monument** (see page 40) and a set of piers stationed at the top end of *sois* (narrow lanes) running off Sukhumvit Road. Indeed, if you are staying in the Sukhumvit area the canal boats are a very useful way of getting across to Khao San Road. A canal boat ride on the east side of the river is an interesting experience and gets you close to ordinary Bangkok life.

Above: *Water taxis plying Bangkok's canals.*

Khlong Tours of Thonburi

⌨ www.realasia.net or
⌨ www.bangkok.com/tours

💰 Tours vary from around B1300 to B1800. Expect to pay around B1000 or less for a two-hour rental of a long-tailed boat – no more than B500 for a one-hour – to explore Thonburi. Fares on the long-tailed taxis that ply the canals on the east bank are B6–15 (have coins ready).

National Museum
✉ Na Phrathat Rd
☎ 022 241 370
🕐 Wed–Sun 09:00–
16:00 (closed on
public holidays)
🚤 Tha Chang pier
🚌 503, 506, 507,
80, 82, 91
🚕 B35
🍴 Café, ice-cream
parlour, shop
🖥 www.thailand
museum.com
Tours: at 09:30 every
Wed and Fri (English);
Wed and Thu (French);
first and second Wed of
the month (German).

Below: *An astonish-
ing collection of
Thai art and culture
is on display at the
National Museum.*

⚜ See Map B–A3	★★★

NATIONAL MUSEUM

The various galleries focus on different his-
torical periods so it may help to first take a
look at the **Gallery of Thai History** for an
overall perspective. The priceless exhibits in
the southern wing – the **Asian Art Gallery**
and, upstairs, the **Dvaravati Art Gallery** –
that cover India, China, Java, Burma, Laos
and Cambodia. Here you will find outstand-
ing examples of prehistoric rock art, early
Buddha images from India, Hindu deities and
superb artefacts from the Dvaravati kingdom
of the 6th to 12th centuries. There are also
two rooms devoted to **Lopburi art**, named
after the town in central Thailand that
became the regional centre of Khmer rule
between the 10th and 13th centuries.

The northern wing has a visually splendid
collection of royal funeral chariots, but the
rooms of enduring artistic interest are those
devoted to the **Sukhothai** and **Ayutthaya**
periods. Sukhothai culture (from the mid-
13th to the late 14th century) created many
of the most exquisite examples of Thai art
and produced the unique form of the
Walking Buddha, shown here
in one particularly notable
example. The museum's mod-
est and inexpensive little café is
situated in this wing – a place
to rest, eat or drink before
moving on to the group of
galleries that separate the
northern and southern wings.

The central wing was originally built at the end of the
18th century as a special palace

National Museum

⭐ See Map B–A3	★★★

for the 'Second King, the next in line to the throne'. **Rama V** abolished this bit of royal nomenclature in 1887 and used the empty rooms to house the art and antiques collected by his father, Rama IV, and previously kept inside the Grand Palace. The rooms are interesting to wander through – it hardly matters in what order you work your way through them – and gaze at whatever takes your fancy in the eclectic collections of exhibits. The **Transportation Gallery** contains elephant seats, and the nearby **Old Weapons Room**, with its colossal model of an armed elephant, is another reminder of the importance of elephants.

Above: *One of the magnificent royal funeral chariots, requiring hundreds of men to pull it, at the National Museum.*

If you work your way through the central wing in the direction of the museum entrance there is one last gallery that should be seen. This is the **Budhhaisawan Chapel**, a beautifully ornamented hall with an ornately decorated roof, lacquered window shutters and fascinating murals depicting scenes from the life of the Buddha and a multitude of devilish figures and benign divinities. Pride of place, though, is reserved for the finely proportioned **Phra Sihing Buddha**. This indisputably superb example of Sukhothai art has a legend that associates it with Sri Lanka but it ended up in Chiang Mai in northern Thailand and from here it was brought to Bangkok by Rama I at the end of the 18th century.

This world-class museum has too much to do justice to on a single visit and it may be best to restrict yourself to just a selection of rooms or, if time allows, make a return trip.

> **Highlights in the National Museum**
> • Vejayant Rajarot funeral chariot
> • Sukhothai sculptures
> • Phra Sihing Buddha (in the Budhhaisawan Chapel)
> • The Red House (Tamnak Daeng)

Above: *The entrance to the Lipstick Club, one of Bangkok's many adult clubs.*

☼ See Map C   ★★★

PATPONG

Patpong, the name of two small streets that run off Silom Rd (see page 71), has become Bangkok's best known **red-light entertainment area**. A visit here will not be every one's idea of a highlight but the place has become enormously popular. The street market in Patpong 1, quite frankly, is over-rated. There is a lot of shoddy merchandise for sale and nearly everything here can be purchased, usually at a better price, at Chatuchak (*see* page 15) or along Silom Road, but there is an intense atmosphere and it can be fun.

The less salubrious side to Patpong is hard to miss because as you make your way through the crowds you will be constantly importuned by touts proffering menus of sex shows on offer. The genealogy of all this lies in the **Vietnam War** when American airbases were established in Thailand and servicemen on leave flocked to Bangkok. Patpong was a Chinese property-owner of an area where affluent Thais were catered for in nightclubs and this attracted one enterprising American who established a bar here. What began as one nightclub for soldiers mushroomed into a lucrative trade in sex and alcohol. The really sleazy bars tend to be tucked away in the *sois* running off Patpong I and 2. More public are the venues where visitors of both sexes are entertained with shows of dubious value. Far more interesting night-time spots are to be found along nearby Silom 4.

Patpong
⊠ Patpong 1 and Patpong 2
M Si Lom
🚇 Sala Daeng (Exit S2)
🍽 Le Bouchon (*see* page 70), Café Di Roma (*see* page 70)

See Map B–A2   ★★★

ROYAL BARGES NATIONAL MUSEUM

Many visitors to Bangkok never set foot on the west bank of the Chao Phraya River but this is one good reason to make the short journey. The special barges on display were used by royalty when making trips along the river and were constructed for maximum visual impact. With a crew of some fifty oarsmen for the largest vessel, they could travel at a stately speed. All the barges are carefully maintained and, on special occasions, some are still floated for ceremonial use.

The **Suphannahongsa**, dating back to the early 20th century, is the most lavishly crafted and decorated of the barges. It was reserved for Rama VI, and little expense was spared in its construction and gilded decoration. The *Suphannahongsa* is carved out of one solid trunk of teakwood and the prow ends in the finely crafted shape of a swan that gives the barge its name, the Golden Swan. Almost just as impressive is the **Anantainagaraj**, the prow of which is graced by the figure of the mythical, seven-headed *naga* (a serpent featured in Hindu and Buddhist iconography). The barges you seen are based on the designs of those that were in service when the Thai capital was up-river at Ayutthaya and the most recent addition to the collection is one built for the golden jubilee of the present king in 1996.

The Royal Barges National Museum features as part of most canal tours, but it is easy to organize your own way there and it can be more fun.

Royal Barges National Museum
✉ Klong Bangkok Noi
☎ 024 240 004
🕐 09:00–17:00 daily
💰 B30
⛴ Tha Phra Pin Klao pier, or a cross-river ferry from Tha Phra Athit pier to Tha Phra Pin Klao. From Tha Phra Pin Klao pier, walk straight ahead and turn at the first left, Soi Wat Duistaram; signs to the museum indicate the way.
🚌 507, 7, 503, 3, 511, 11, 509, 9 (get off at the first bus stop over the Pin Klao Bridge)

Below: *The gracious setting of the Royal Barges National Museum.*

Suan Pakkard Palace
✉ 352–4 Sri
Ayutthaya Rd
☎ 022 454 934
🕐 09:00–16:00 daily
🚇 Phaya Thai
🚌 13, 18, 38
ℹ B100 (guided
tours in English are
available free of
charge)
🖥 www.suanpakkad.
com

Below: *Unlike at
Jim Thompson's
Museum, visitors
can freely wander
around and inside
the charming Thai
houses at Suan
Pakkard Palace.*

See Map B–G3 ★★★

SUAN PAKKARD PALACE

This set of traditional Thai houses with gardens, originally built in northern Thailand, was moved to Bangkok by the late **Prince and Princess Chumphot** over fifty years ago, at a time when the site they chose was a cabbage farm (the literal translation of Suan Pakkard). The royal couple lived in the houses and over the years filled them with art and artefacts and turned the rough land into the handsome gardens you see today.

There are priceless examples of Khmer art, precious **statues** from the 7th to the 14th century and everyday items like **betel-nut boxes** (for holding nuts of the areca palm that are chewed with betel leaves as a mild narcotic), **porcelain** and other **ceramics**. There are also Bronze Age exhibits from **Ban Chiang**, a major site in the northeast of the country. You will also come across European art like a fine set of French drawings from the 17th century. The highlight of any visit is the **Lacquer Pavilion**, a beautiful construct on stilts from the Ayutthaya region, decorated inside with stunning lacquer paintings in black and gold, depicting scenes from the *Ramayana* and the life of the Buddha.

What lends especial charm to Suan Pakkard are the landscaped gardens where you can wander around and forget the pulsating metropolis that surrounds this little oasis of peace.

⛟ *See Map B–G4*   ★★

SIAM SQUARE

Not only is Siam Square not a square, it lacks a focal point. Despite this, the conglomeration of streets, *sois*, Skytrain station, covered walkways, steel-and-glass buildings and smaller shops that make up Siam Square come close to being the heart of the city. It is a central link in the Skytrain system, the place where the two lines meet and therefore a crossover point on journeys across Bangkok. From Siam station, a covered walkway takes you westward to the giant **MBK Centre** (see page 52), a major shopping destination, while in the other direction the walkway leads to the busy junction where the main road, Rama I, meets Ratchadamri Rd. This junction is dominated by the **Central World Plaza** and the exciting little **Erawan shrine** (see page 36).

At night, Siam Square is lit up with neon and acts like a magnet to the city's young population. Of the two main buildings, visitors are usually drawn to the **Siam Discovery Centre** with its plush retail outlets and sophisticated cineplex on the top floor (see page 72). The other building, the **Siam Centre**, has less swanky shops. Day and night, young Thais love to mingle, shop and eat in the maze of little streets across the road and this is where fashion-conscious teenagers come to buy clothes and accessories. It can be interesting because it is so Thai in character and even the international-style Novotel hotel that is situated here has a frenzied atmosphere all of its own.

Above: *Siam Square's ugly urban architecture hides a consumer's paradise of retail outlets and the largest store of all, the MBK Centre, is reached by a walkway from the Skytrain.*

Siam Square
✉ Rama I Rd
🚉 Siam
🚌 15, 47, 79, 25, 29, 508

See Map B–A4 | ★★

Above: *The grounds of Wat Arun offer a quiet place for a relaxed stroll.*

WAT ARUN

River tours (*see page 21*) nearly all include a visit to Wat Arun, so at times the temple becomes a little crowded with visitors, but there are frequent cross-river ferries from Thai Thien pier so it easy to make your own way there.

This most famous of *wats* (temples) is on the west side of the river because Taksin (*see page 78*) chose this bank for the site of the new capital after the fall of Ayutthaya. The location of Wat Arun, where an older temple already stood, was chosen by Taksin as the ground for his palace and the Emerald Buddha (*see page 16*) was kept in the original temple until Rama I made the big move to the east side of the Chao Phraya. The two kings who succeeded him, Rama II and III, appreciated the symbolic value of the origi-

Wat Arun
✉ Arun Amarin Rd, Thonburi (west side of Chao Phraya River)
☎ 024 663 167
🕐 07:00–17:00 daily
🚤 A ferry across the river from Thai Thien pier
💲 B20

WAT ARUN

☆ *See* Map B–A4 **★★**

Demons and Demigods
Wat Arun was designed to represent Mount Meru, the Mount Olympus of Khmer mythology, and statues of various mythological figures adorn the interior. Some are half-human and half-bird in appearance and these are the *kinnari* that support the different levels; others are pure demons, the *yaksha*.

nal temple, now called the **Temple of Dawn** because apparently that was the time of day when Taksin chose the site for his palace, and had it rebuilt in the unique style that you see today.

The central tower (114m high), the *prang*, and the four smaller ones around it glitter in the sunshine to startling effect and you will see why when up close to the temple, a vast number of pieces of porcelain having been laid into the stucco to form the sun-catching outlines of flowers. The mythical figures that also decorate the structure are *kinnari* (half-female, half-bird) and *yaksha* (devils).

You can ascend the steep stairs for soul-stirring views of the Chao Phraya River – the Grand Palace is not difficult to pick out – and the opportunity to see the patterned porcelain in detail. When you reach the first level you are close to a set of four *mondops*, squarish little houses containing statues of the Buddha, placed to face north, south, east and west. Up on the next level there are more statues, this time of the Hindu god Indra.

Left: *A row of golden Buddhas at Wat Arun; the main Buddha image inside the chapel is said to have been designed by Rama II.*

☆ *See* Map B–B4 ★★

Wat Pho
⊠ Two entrances: Thai Wang Rd and Soi Chetuphon
🕓 08:00–18:00 daily
🚉 Tha Tien pier (turn right onto Minaret Rd and then left for Soi Chetuphon; straight on from the pier exit for Thai Wang Rd
🚌 1, 6, 7, 8, 12, 44, 508, 512
💰 B20
💻 www.watpho.com

WAT PHO

The chief attraction of Wat Pho is the stupendous **Reclining Buddha**. The temple was founded during the Ayutthaya period centuries before Bangkok became the capital. It is very close to the Grand Palace and a combined visit is possible if you just want to pop in and see the Reclining Buddha. To appreciate Wat Pho as a whole, however, a separate visit is best, because the temple compound is large and there are many galleries surrounding the *ubosot*, the main sanctuary. The Reclining Buddha is in its own chapel near the entrance on Thai Wang Rd.

King Rama III ordered the building of a special chapel to house the Reclining Buddha and it seems that a much larger chamber was needed to do justice to the monumental scale of the figure. The Buddha, in a state of bliss and about to enter nirvana, is 45m (148ft) long and 15m (49ft) high. It is made of bricks and plaster but what you see is a holy giant smiling enigmatically, covered in gold leaf and with 108 auspicious signs inlaid with mother-of-pearl on the soles of his feet. The long gilded earlobes signify the Buddha's noble birth – he was born the son of a king.

Use the entrance on Soi Chetuphon so as to wander through the galleries and the *ubosot* before making your way over to the east side to gaze at the Reclining Buddha, and then exit onto

Below: *The temple compound of Wat Pho, first constructed in the 16th century and rebuilt by Rama I in 1781.*

WAT PHO

See Map B–B4 ★★

Thai Wang Road. Numerous galleries surround the *ubosot* on its four sides, filled with countless statues that were brought to Bangkok from the older capital of Ayutthaya by Rama I. The main sanctuary itself is graced by a wall and a set of finely decorated teak-

wood doors – a work of art in their own right – lavishly illustrated with scenes from the *Ramayana*, India's Homeric-style epic that came to Thailand under the influence of the Khmers and established itself firmly in the national consciousness. Part of the story of the *Ramakien*, the Thai name for the *Ramayana*, is told in detail in the 150 or so marble reliefs around the base of the sanctuary wall. The interior is another visual extravaganza with a brightly painted ceiling and colossal pillars. The elaborate central altar shines in gold, home to a bronze image of the Buddha from Ayutthaya.

From the sanctuary, thread your way through the temple compound to the Reclining Buddha. Along the way there is plenty to see in the form of variously sized *chedis*, small towers containing relics. There are four large, gaudy-looking ones, covered in ceramic tiles, that commemorate the first four Bangkok kings.

Wat Pho is also a centre for **traditional medicine** and you will pass the pavilion where massage training courses are conducted. As a day visitor, you can opt for an authentic Thai massage, at B300 for an hour, which will certainly recharge your batteries.

Above: *The head of the Reclining Buddha, like the rest of the body, is covered with gold leaf and lacquer.*

Wat Pho
Wat Pho is the oldest temple in the city and, since the time of Rama III, the largest as well. Like all Thai temples, the holiest building is the ordination hall or *ubosoth*. Commonly shortened to *bot*, this building is situated in the inner courtyard and is usually highly decorated, often with murals serving an educational purpose.

See Map B–D1 ★

Above : *Vimanmek Palace, the world's largest teak mansion.*

VIMANMEK PALACE

This teakwood palace was originally built on Ko Chang, east of Bangkok, but Rama V had it taken apart and moved to the Dusit area of Bangkok where it was reassembled in 1901. The king, who spent a large part of the next five years living in Vimanmek Palace, was keen to develop Dusit as a area of European-style sophistication.

The guided tour escorts you around 30 or so rooms and highlights a selection of the contents, noting the fact that this was the first Thai residence to install an interior shower. The interior of the palace has been lavishly restored and the overall effect – an artful blending of traditional Thai elegance with modern comforts – is very much in keeping with Rama V's aspirations.

Reaching Dusit requires a stiff walk from the boat pier or Skytrain station – you can catch a taxi from either – so while you are here it is worth seeing the other buildings open to the public. The **Abhisek Dusit Throne Hall**, at the back of the palace, is now an exhibition hall with displays of fine arts and crafts; there are excellent **carvings** from soapstone and wood, **textiles**, **neilloware** and beautiful **gold** and **silverware**. You can wander around at will and appreciate the talent of craftspeople from rural communities across Thailand.

Vimanmek Palace
✉ Ratchawithi Rd
☎ 026 286 300
🕐 09:30–16:00 daily
🚆 Phaya Thai
🚤 Tha Thewet pier
🚌 10, 56, 70, 72, 510
💰 B100 (but free with your ticket to the Grand Palace)
Tours
Compulsory, every half hour
Dance Shows
Traditional Thai dance
🕐 daily at 10:30 and 14:00
Dress Code
As for the Grand Palace (see page 16)
💻 www.vimanmek. com

☆ See Map B–D4 ★

WAT MANGKON KAMALAWAT

This temple is a major centre of worship for the Thai-Chinese in Bangkok and it has a panache all of its own. This is partly due to its setting in the heart of Chinatown and there is a strong Chinese inflection to the **Buddhist iconography** on show, not least in the bursts of primary colours that characterize the statues of the deities.

The temple is invariably busy with people hurrying in for an act of devotion. Flowers are a popular donation, along with incense, and visitors will learn a lot about the everyday religious practices of devout Thai-Chinese. The temple functions like an oracle, with worshippers on their knees vigorously shaking narrow pieces of bamboo filled with small slips of paper. The piece that is eventually shaken loose is the prophetic answer to the proffered question.

Look for the four large statues that guard the main entrance to the temple. They create a stern presence, relieved by the calm atmosphere of the main chapel and its array of pacific Buddhas. Lanterns contribute to the meditative mood and complement the characteristic reds of a Chinese temple.

In the vicinity of Wat Mangkon Kamalawat lies the hustle and bustle of Chinatown and nearby shops retail temple paraphernalia in the form of paper for ritual burning, packages of fruits and flowers, and incense.

Wat Mangkon Kamalawat
✉ Charoen Krung Rd
🕐 07:00–18:00 daily
Ⓜ Hua Lamphong
🚢 Ratchawongse pier
🚆 Hua Lamphong
🅿 Free
🍴 the Grand China Princess Hotel (see page 59) has a useful café on the second floor as well as a daily buffet lunch.

Below: *You are never alone in Wat Mangkon Kamalawat and the flow of human traffic seems more suited to a railway station than a temple.*

☆ *See* Map B–C3 | ★

Wat Suthat and the Giant Swing
✉ junction of Bamrung Muang Rd and Ti Thong Rd
🕐 09:00–21:00 daily
🚏 Tha Phanfa canal boat pier
🚌 30, 15, 47, 79 (from Siam Square to Democracy Monument), followed by a 10-minute walk
💰 B20

WAT SUTHAT AND THE GIANT SWING

Wat Suthat dates to the mid-19th century, although building work began more than fifty years earlier. The *viharn*, the central assembly hall or chapel, is home to a highly revered Buddha image, **Phra Buddha Sakyamuni**. This huge 14th-century statue was brought from Sukhothai, a river journey of over 400km. The surrounding murals depict the various incarnations of the Buddha and are finely executed works of art. The carvings on the immense doors are the work of anonymous but highly talented craftsmen employed by Rama II. There are over 150 more images of the Buddha in the galleries around the *viharn*, while in the courtyard there are statues of Chinese sages and other anomalous figures.

Outside the temple, red-painted posts are what remain of the **Giant Swing**, *Sao Ching Cha*, that once dominated this position. Competing groups of men would take turns to swing from an open seat suspended between the posts in an attempt to grab with their teeth a bag of gold coins that hung from a nearby, 25m post. It was a dangerous endeavour and serious accidents were not uncommon before the spectacle was brought to an end in the 1930s.

Bamrung Muang Road, the main street, is worth exploring for its multitude of shops.

Below: *Bangkok's tallest viharn is to be found at Wat Suthat.*

WAT TRAIMIT

The entrance to this temple does not draw attention to itself and were it not for the organized groups milling about on the pavement outside you would most likely pass straight by when looking for it. Such, though, is the fame of the temple's solid gold Buddha that you are unlikely to be alone on your visit; keep a close watch on your belongings. The **Golden Buddha**, one of the most photographed figures in Bangkok, is over 3m (10ft) high and ranks as the largest solid gold Buddha in the world, weighing in at well over five tons. Equally remarkable is an apparent lack of security about the place, though the sheer size of the Buddha probably protects it from robbers.

This Buddha is a fine example of Sukhothai art, and the splendour of the gold is extraordinary. The figure dates back to the 13th century and when Rama III brought it to Bangkok it was admired solely for its artistic value, the gold being having been hidden beneath a stucco surface to protect it from thieves. It was not until the mid-1950s, when a decision was made to relocate the Buddha to Wat Traimit, that it accidentally fell in the process of being transported and a crack appeared in the stucco. A gleam of gold was detected and the plaster was removed to reveal the treasure hidden beneath. The story of the discovery is told briefly in display cases alongside the Golden Buddha.

Most city tours take in a visit to Wat Traimit but it is within walking distance of Hua Lamphong station, so you can make your own way there.

Above: *The solid gold Buddha in Wat Traimit is appropriately located in Chinatown, the very heart of Bangkok's gold trade.*

Wat Traimit
✉ Traimit Rd, where Yaowarat Rd meets Charoen Krung Rd
🕐 09:00–17:00 daily
M Hua Lamphong
🚌 25,53
💲 B20

Above: *The Erawan shrine is never empty during the day and a small troupe of Thai dancers often performs here.*

Practical Buddhism

Nearly 95 per cent of Thailand's people call themselves Buddhists and this is reflected in the multitude of shrines and temples to be found in the capital. For Thais, it is a highly practical religion and the devotees seen at the Erawan shrine, for example, are not there in the hope of attaining a state of nirvana but, more likely, to hopefully secure good exam results for their children or success in some new venture.

Temples and Shrines

Erawan

A colourful and often busy little shrine in the heart of the city, the Erawan shrine is easy to locate because it is next to the Grand Hyatt Erawan and a couple of minutes' walk from Chit Lom Station. A stream of Bangkok residents call in throughout the day, with offerings of garlands, and in the evening there is nearly always a small band of dancers performing to the accompaniment of live music. The scene is especially fascinating because of the bizarre context: traffic roaring past on the street and the Skytrain gliding by overhead while devotees pay homage and give thanks at a colourful, modestly-sized shrine to a Hindu god by the side of the pavement. The origin of Erawan is related to the nearby hotel and a number of accidents that occurred during its construction work. The resident spirit, it seems, was perturbed by the disturbances and in order to placate the spirit's wrath this shrine was erected as a form of compensation. ⊠ *junction of Rama I Rd and Ratchadamri Rd,* 🚈 *Chit Lom (Exit E1)*

Wat Benchamabophit

The best reason for making a visit here is to see for yourself the daily donation of alms to Buddhist monks by citizens of the city. The catch is that you need to reach **Nakhon Pathom**, the street by the temple that runs parallel to Thanon Rama V, before 07:00 to be sure of witnessing the proceedings. The temple itself, also known as the **White Marble** because of the colour of the building material, displays a fetching combination of traditional Thai and European features and there is a host of Buddha images in the temple's courtyard.

✉ *Sri Ayudhaya Rd and Rama V Rd,*
🕐 *07:00–17:00 daily*
🎫 *B20,* 🚈 *Phaya Thai (and then a taxi)*
🚢 *a walk from Tha Thewet pier,*
🚌 *10, 56, 70, 72, 510*

Wat Rachanada

Wat Rachanada is not your typical Thai temple – no shimmering spires and gold-leaf statues – but this pink-fronted edifice is certainly eye-catching. There are 37 pitch black spires, and the temple's interior is decidedly strange. It consists of a bewildering set of narrow corridors that head off in all directions and a spiral staircase that seems to go on for

ever. Outside the temple, to one side of the car park, there is a self-proclaimed **Buddha Centre** with numerous stalls selling amulets and garish statues of figures from Hindu mythology. From Democracy Monument (*see page 21*), it is a short walk along Ratchadamnoen Klang Rd to a busy traffic junction where Wat Rachanada stands on the right side of the road. To reach the entrance, though, follow the sign for the temple down Maha Chai Rd and you will come to a courtyard area on your right.

✉ *junction of Maha Chai Rd and Ratchadamnoen Klang Rd,*

Below: *Wat Benchamabophit's Kafka-esque interior comes as a complete surprise given its conventional exterior.*

🕐 *09:00–17:00 daily,*
💰 *Free*
🚋 *a walk from Tha Phra Athit pier,* 🚌 *30 15, 47, 79;* **Canal Boat Transport:** *Tha Phanfa*

Wat Saket and the Golden Mount

When Rama I ordered the building of Wat Saket, it lay outside the city walls that defended Bangkok, and it was Rama III who consolidated the temple's importance by adding a reliquary for some teeth of the Buddha. The *chedi*, however, was not well constructed and it later collapsed; what you see now was built under Rama V. It is a short walk to the top of the hill and from the top there are splendid views over the metropolis. A visit to Wat Saket, close to the Tha Phanfa canal boat pier, could be taken in before or after seeing Wat Rachanada, a short and signposted walk separating the two temples.

✉️ *Boriphat Rd*
☎️ *022 234 561*
🕐 *07:30–17:30 daily*
💰 *Free,* 🚋 *a walk from Tha Phra Athit pier;* **Canal Boat Transport:** *Tha Phanfa*

Green Spaces
Lumphini Park

At some time or other you will be driven to escape the noise and intensity of Bangkok and a stroll around Lumphini Park beats staring at the television in a hotel room. It is almost eerie to find yourself surrounded by green space and relative silence and the park is big enough that the best part of an hour is occupied walking around it.

Below: *A climb to the top of Wat Saket gains one access to the golden* chedi, *from where there are panoramic views of the city.*

There are two lakes, with pedalos and rowing boats for hire (B30 per half hour), a children's playground, open-air swimming pool and gym, and picnic tables dotted about (a food Court opens in the evening). From early February onwards you will see kites being flown everywhere. The main entrance, marked by a statue of the king who donated the park to the city's residents, is a short walk from the Skytrain or Silom Metro station.

⊠ Rama IV Rd
M Silom or Lumphini,
🚌 2, 4, 5, 7, 15, 47;
🚤 Sala Daeng

Sanam Luang

This park has a great location, close to the **Royal Grand Palace**, and the vista is more impressive than Lumphini Park although it is nowhere near as large. Both greens attract kite-flyers between late February and early May, especially at weekends. Sanam Luang is the site for two very different formal occasions: royal cremation ceremonies and the annual **Ploughing Ceremony**. The time for a cremation is left to fate but the actual day in May for the Ploughing Ceremony is ascertained annually by astrologists anxious to fix the best possible date and time, the ceremony marking the beginning of a new rice season.

⊠ Ratchadamnoen Nai Rd,
🚤 Tha Phra pier,
🚌 3, 6, 7, 8, 9, 12, 25, 30, 32, 47, 53;
🚤 Phaya Thai (and then a taxi)

Other Attractions
Democracy Monument

This Monument dates back to 1940 when its four angel wings, aspiring to a height of 24m (79ft), were unveiled to commemorate Thailand's achieving the status of a constitutional monarchy eight years earlier. This, plus the fact that the city's university is not too far away, helps explain why the site has become the epicentre for protests against military rule. In October 1973 there were massive protests here which resulted in many fatalities and there were similar acts of brutality against protesters in 1992. Today, the monument serves as a useful reference point in this part of the city (see panel, page 40).

⊠ Ratchadamnoen Klang Rd, 🚤 Tha Phra Athit pier and walk through Khao San Rd, 🚌 30 15, 47, 79; **Canal Boat Transport:** Tha Phanfa pier

Silom Road

There is no 'must see' attraction along Silom Road and it is easy to miss out if not staying in the area, but the ease of reaching this visitor-friendly street of shops and restaurants makes a visit worthwhile. The road runs from near the river up

Above: *Democracy Monument, designed in 1939 by Italian sculptor Corrado Feroci.*

Democracy Monument

Neither the Skytrain nor Metro reaches the area to the northwest of the Grand Palace but there are various attractions in this part of the city – Wat Benchamabophit, Wat Rachanada, Wat Saket and the Golden Mount (*see* page 38) and Vimanmek Palace (*see* page 32) – and Democracy Monument serves as a useful orientation and transport point. It can be reached in a short walk from Khao San Road (*see* page 14). A number of city buses from Siam Square also pass by Democracy Monument.

to Patpong (*see* page 24) and there are good shopping and eating facilities at both ends. In the middle section of Silom Road stands the colourful **Sri Mariamman Hindu temple**.

M *Silom (top end)*
🚤 *Tha Sathon (Central Pier) or Oriental Pier*
🛥 *Saphan Taksin (for the river end); Chong Nonsi (the middle); Sala Daeng (top end)*

Queen Saovabha Memorial Institute (Snake Farm)

This is a professionally run and respected herpetological institute, founded in 1920 as the

Pasteur Institute and now managed by the Thai Red Cross. **Snake milking** sessions are open daily to the public and begin with an instructive slide-show about how to deal with snake bites. Some of the snakes you see having their venom extracted are among the world's most dangerous creatures but the handlers know what they are doing.

✉ *junction of Rama IV Rd and Henri Dunant Rd*
☎ *022 520 161*
🕐 *Snake milking at 10:30 and 14:00 Mon–Fri; 10:30 Sat and Sun,* 💰 *B70,* **M** *Sam Yan,* 🛥 *Sala Daeng*

ACTIVITIES
A Walk Through Chinatown

Take a Chao Phraya Express boat to the Ratchawongse pier and walk about 300m up Ratchawong Rd until you reach a zebra crossing and the narrow, pedestrianized **Sampeng Lane**. It is easy to miss Sampeng Lane – if you reach a set of traffic lights then you have – but look for people entering and leaving what looks like a tiny alleyway.

Turn right into Sampeng Lane and you are immediately in the heart of **Chinatown**, swamped by people and surrounded by ancient-looking shops displaying a bewildering array of items for sale.

Sampeng Lane runs parallel with the main road, Yaowarat Road, and you can turn down any lane on your left and make your way through to this traffic-congested road. Try to stay on Sampeng Lane until you reach Itsaranuphap (Soi 16) and go left, because it passes *Talaat Kao*, the Old Market, on your right as you make your way down Soi 16.

Yaowarat Road is Chinatown's main drag and the constant stream of traffic is off-putting but there is plenty to see, especially gold shops. Many of the old buildings, their colours faded and balconies tottering, seem to be living on borrowed time; waiting to be renovated, they preserve

> **Veggie-fest**
> Chinatown's annual Vegetarian Festival takes place around Sep–October, the first nine days of the ninth lunar month, and all the restaurants offer special non-meat dishes. Wat Mangkon Kamalawat becomes busier than ever and a mood of festivity enlivens the temple.

Below: *Demons and devils – these two are representations in fabric – abound in Chinatown's temples.*

Above: *Yaowarat Road, the main thoroughfare in Chinatown, is packed with gold shops – and traffic.*

palpable echoes of the 1930s when they would have been in their prime.

You can walk straight across Yaowarat Road and continue on Soi 16 until it becomes Soi 21 after crossing another main road, Charoen Krung Road. Here you can visit **Wat Mangkon Kamalawat** (*see* page 33).

Retrace your steps to Yaowarat Road and turn right, walking along this busy street until you reach Thanon Ratchawong on your left, just after the Shangri-La Restaurant. This takes you back to the pier. Alternatively, stay on Yaowarat Road and take a rest at the Grand China Princess Hotel where there is a lunch buffet (11:30–14:30 daily) and a café on the second floor (open until 21:00).

Guided Tours

Travel companies offering guided tours of the city and short excursions from the capital are not hard to find. They can be useful if your stay is a short one because travelling around Bangkok is usually a very time-consuming business; the drawback to many tours is that they include places you may not want to see and insist on visits to other commercialized attractions like the floating markets in Thonburi. Their websites have details of itineraries, prices and further information.

Real Asia offers more authentic and off-beat tours than any other company in

Bangkok and can be recommended to anyone with a sense of adventure or curiosity. Their Amazing Bangkok Cyclist Tour (see page 48) is especially noteworthy and good feedback is coming from their Train Tour that gets you out of the city, but not to the usual destinations of Kanchanaburi or Ayutthaya. Thai cooking courses are also available. ⊠ 10/5-7 Soi 26 Sukhumvit Rd, ☎ 027 129 301, 💻 www.realasia.net

Bangkok's Smiling Tours runs a number of tours: the Grand Palace, Temple and City, Canal Tour, Floating Market, Bangkok by Night, Safari World, Kanchanaburi and Ayutthaya. Rates vary depending on the numbers involved. ☎ 018 273 815, 💻 www.bangkoksmiling.com

More Thailand, an online travel agency. 💻 www.morethailand.com

Thai Cookery Classes

The best-value Thai cooking classes in Bangkok are the vegetarian ones run by **May Kaidee** from her restaurant. Classes kick off at 09:00 with a visit to the local market for fresh ingredients and an hour later you are in the kitchen getting down to the business of cooking. ⊠ 123 Tanao Rd, ☎ 022 817 137, 🚤 Tha Phra Athit boat pier (N13) and then a walk through Khao San Rd., 💻 www.maykaidee.com

The Landmark is not the only Bangkok hotel to offer cooking classes but if the dishes at the hotel's Nipa Thai restaurant (*see* page 66) are anything to go by

Below: *Tuk-tuks will take you on a tour of Bangkok's busy streets.*

Above: *Thai cookery classes are easy to book in Bangkok, and lessons are always in English.*

then this would be a good place to learn how to concoct those fiery Thai curries. Famous dishes like *tom yam goong* (spicy soup with lemon grass and prawns) and *mussaman gai* (a mild and sweet curry) are taught and the course fee includes a meal at the restaurant. One- and five-day courses available. ⊠ The Landmark Hotel, 138 Sukhumvit Rd, ☎ 022 540 404 ext. 4305, 🚇 Nana.

Massages, Health & Beauty

Spas offering massages and various forms of health and beauty treatments are everywhere in Bangkok and it is a matter of finding the treatment and the price that suits your needs. The sois off Sukhumvit are a prime hunting ground for comparing prices and nearly all the four- and fiver-star hotels have their in-house spas, many of which are open to non-residents.

Banyan Tree Spa is one of the more sophisticated and expensive spas in the city, offering massages for most parts of the body and a tempting range of beauty treatments designed to pamper your skin, bones and ego. Prices are set in US dollars and vary from $70 to $155, depending on the time and treatment, but couples can benefit from a discount if they take the same program. ⊠ Banyan Tree Hotel, 21/100 Sathorn Street, ☎ 026 791 200, ⏰ 10:00–19:00 daily, **M** Lumphini, 🖳 www.banyantreespa.com

Goodwill has been recommended by more than one visitor to Bangkok as a

Dental Hospital
If you require emergency dental treatment or specialist attention for a particular problem – dentures, oral surgery, root canal work – the Dental Hospital is the place to go. Ordinary fillings and examinations are also available.
⊠ Soi 49, 88/88 Sukhumvit Rd
☎ 022 605 000
⏰ 09:00–20:00 daily
🚇 Phrom Phong
🖳 www.dental hospitalbangkok.com

pleasant little place that delivers good-value massages and body treatments in an attractive setting. There is a garden café on the rooftop and the little restaurant area serves vegetarian meals. Haircuts and styling, as well as facials, manicures and pedicures, plus a range of massages. Prices for massages average about B500, haircuts and styling from B150 to B5000 while facials average B1500. ⊠ 44/16 Convent Rd (opposite a hospital), ☎ 026 320 626, ⊕ 10:00–22:00 Mon–Sat, 🔲 Sala Daeng.

Instead of offering the usual gamut of body treatments, **Let's Relax** sticks to foot and body massages. The downstairs area is the most attractive but the body massages all take place upstairs. The price for combined foot reflexology and massage is B2200, lasting over two hours in total. ⊠ 77 Sukhumvit Soi 39, ☎ 026 626 935, ⊕ 09:00–18:30 daily, 🔲 Phrom Phong.

Alternative Health

Balavi Natural Health Centre offers alternative courses of treatment, in the form of physical therapy, diet programmes, colon cleansing, acupuncture, for a host of

Convent Dental Centre
Dental clinics offering inexpensive but professional treatment are readily available in Bangkok and the Convent Dental Centre is typical of its kind. Straightforward fillings are B250 and the range of cleaning and polishing, whitening and bleaching treatments are all clearly priced.
⊠ 36/2 Convent Rd,
☎ 026 322 794,
⊕ 09:00–20:00 daily
🔲 Sala Daeng

Left: *Skyline pool and spa at the Banyan Tree Hotel.*

Above: *Thai massage parlours are particularly plentiful in the Sukhumvit Road area.*

bodily ailments like allergies, obesity and insomnia. ⊠ 191/3 Soi Ranong, Rama VI Road, ☎ 022 795 658, ⏰ 08:30–20:00 Mon–Fri; 08:30–17:30 Sat, 🚉 Nana, 🖳 www.balavi.com

A little bit of everything is available at **G2B Integrated Medicine Clinic**, from blood analysis to meditation, based on a holistic approach that takes in detoxification, massages and colonics. ⊠ 3/F, room 315, The Landmark Plaza, 138 Sukhumvit Rd, ☎ 022 558 407, ⏰ 09:00–18:00 Tue–Sun (closed Mon), 🖳 www.g2bclinic.com

St Carlos Medical Spa is an 'east meets west' spa that incorporates a clinic, using natural products, herbal medicine, detoxification and fasting for health and well-being. Skin care, sleep problems and weight loss are catered for, with all treatments based on a preliminary medical check-up. ⊠ 5/84 Moo 2, Tiwanon Rd, Pathumthani, ☎ 029 756 700, ⏰ 07:00–21:00 daily, 🖳 www.stcarlos.com

Fitness and Yoga

Absolute Yoga offers not ordinary yoga but Bikram yoga – in a room with a temperature of 37°C – and Power Vinyasa yoga. The website provides full details and a map showing the precise location. All you need is a change of clothing. A single session costs B500 but there is a discount when booking a set of five classes. ⊠ 14/F Unico Building, Soi Lang Suan, Phloenchit Road, ☎ 026 521 333, ⏰ 09:00–21:00 Mon–Thu, 09:00–20:00 Fri, 09:00–17:00 Sat–Sun,

---

Martial Arts
The Bangkok Fight Club, ⊠ 31/F Serm Mit Tower, Asoke, ☎ 018 462 010, 🖳 www.bangkokfight club.com Established over five years ago, this club has classes at various levels and for both sexes and children in a variety of martial arts, as well as jiujitsu and self-defence. Single lessons cost B400 but there is also a membership fee.

📍 Chit Lom (Exit 4), 🖥 www.absoluteyoga bangkok.com

Clark Hatch Fitness Center offers a gym, yoga, sauna and steam room, aerobic studio, outdoor swimming pool and massages. Daily membership costs B300. ✉ Amari Atrium Hotel, 1880 New Petchburi Road, ☎ 027 182 001, ext 3981, ⊙ 06:30–22:00 Mon–Fri, 08:00–22:00 Sat–Sun, 🖥 www.amari.com

Grand Spa and Fitness Club has daily classes in strenuous forms of yoga; there is a sauna, steam room and a juice bar. Daily membership is B550. ✉ Sheraton Grande Hotel, 250 Sukhumvit Rd, ☎ 026 498 121, ⊙ 05:30–22:00 daily, 🖥 www.starwood hotels.com/sheraton

Yoga Elements is a well-established yoga studio with classes in Vinyasa/Ashtanga yoga and Pilates mat sessions. The cost of a single class starts at B450. ✉ 23/F Vanissa Building, 29 Ploen Chit Road, ☎ 026 555 671, ⊙ 10:00–21:00 daily, 🖥 www.yogaelements.com

Fun for Children

Between February and April, kite-flying at Lumphini Park and Sanam Luang is popular and kites can be purchased in the parks. The Snake Farm (*see* page 40) will fascinate most children.

Children's Discovery Museum

There are lots of buttons to press and experiments to observe, computer screens and puppet shows of the educational kind. To reach the museum, take a taxi from the Metro station to the Queen Sirikit Park. ✉ Kamphaengphet 4 Rd, Chatuchak, ☎ 026 517 333, ⊙ 09:00–17:00 Tue–Fri; 10:00–18:00

Thai Boxing
The atmosphere is feverish, the betting is heavy and the stamina of the young boxers is something to be amazed at. Seat prices vary from B220 to over B1000, but you do not need to be in the front row to enjoy the spectacle; purchase your ticket at least half an hour early. There are two stadiums where Thai boxing competitions take place on a regular basis – Ratchadamnoen Boxing Stadium and Lumphini Stadium – though boxing may be moved out of Lumphini in the near future so check before turning up.
✉ Ratchadamnoen Boxing Stadium: 1 Ratchadamnoen Noi, ☎ 022 814 205, ⊙ 18:00 on Mon, Wed and Thu; 17:00 on Sun. ✉ Lumphini Stadium: Rama IV Rd, ☎ 022 528 765, ⊙ 18:00 Tue and Fri; 17:00 and 20:00 Sun.

Above: *Go with the flow – though only experienced cyclists venture out alone.*

Sat–Sun (closed Mon, except on holidays), 𝖎 B50 (children); B70 (adults), **M** Chatuchak Park, 💻 www.bkkchildrenmuseum.com

Dream World

Suitable for children under 12, this theme park is full of rides and has a daily show at 14:30. It is best visited at the weekend when Disneyland-type cartoon characters stroll about the place. ✉ Rangsit-Ongharak Rd, 8km (5 miles) north of Don Muang Airport, ☎ 025 331 152, ⏰ 10:00–17:00 Mon–Fri; 10:00–19:00 Sat–Sun, 𝖎 B1000, including buffet lunch and rides, **M** Chatuchak Park, 🚤 Mo Chit, 💻 www.dreamworld-th.com

An Activity You Thought You'd Never Do in Bangkok

Cycling on Bangkok's roads may sound life-threatening but it can be done safely and enjoyably and Real Asia's Amazing Bangkok Cyclist Tour is proof of this. The package includes bicycle, drinks and lunch and groups are kept small enough to ensure safety and sociability. The trip across the river to Thonburi is recommended because it takes you out of the urban scene and opens a window on ordinary Bangkok life in a way that will surprise and delight. Equal, if not more, fun is the journey to and from the pier, and your mind will boggle as you find yourself cycling across major road junctions, under concrete highways and through narrow lanes exposing a side of Bangkok rarely experienced by the visitor who keeps his/her feet on the ground. The bike tours depart at 13:00, daily, from ✉ 10/5-7 Soi 26, off Sukhumvit Rd and cost B1500; weekend tours are longer and cost B2000.

Ice Skating

One way of escaping the tropical heat is to be found on the eighth level of the Central World Plaza on Ratchadamri Rd (☎ 022 559 500, ext 2747) at the World Ice Skating Centre. It is open daily from 10:00 to 20:30 at night and the admission fee of B130 includes skate rental. Ice skating lessons are also available.

Left: *For colourful umbrellas like these, and other arts and crafts, head straight for the Suan Lum Night Bazaar (see page 50).*

SHOPPING
Arts & Crafts

As well as the shops listed here, there is also Chatuchak Weekend Market (*see page 15*) to consider for arts and crafts.

Jade Thongtavee

One of the better shops in River City for small gifts and craft items, all made from jade. Prices are marked but expect a small discount. Most of the other shops in this high-octane consumer den specialize in high-priced antiquities and glamorous art and crafts.

⊠ *Rm. 202, 2nd Floor, River City, Trok Rongnamkang, off Charoen Krung Rd* ☎ *022 370 077,*

🕘 *daily from 10:00 to 20:00,* 🚢 *Sri Praya pier*

Jim Thompson's Thai Silk

The main shop is at Jim Thompson's Museum (*see page 18*) but there are smaller outlets around the city. The silk can be purchased by the metre, with the price depending on the quality of the material, but ready-made garments are also available. As well as scarves and dresses, buy items for the home, like seat cushions.

⊠ *Soi Kasem San 2, Rama 1 Rd,* ☎ *022 167 368,* 🚇 *National Stadium,*

💻 *www.jim thompson.com*

Other Outlets at:

⊠ *The Peninsula, 333*

Bargaining

Prices are fixed and usually stay fixed in department stores and shopping malls, but where a price is not displayed take it as read that bargaining is expected and that the first price suggested by the vendor is somewhere between 15% and 80% more than what you might want to pay. The trick is to try and work out whether the first price is close to what is expected or outrageously higher. Once you have made an offer you cannot go lower, and will be expected to go higher, so make sure you begin with this in mind. Places like **Suan Lum Night Bazaar** (*see page 50*) and many of the smaller outlets in MBK (*see page 53*) tend to have prices displayed but a discount of 10%–15% can be expected.

Bangkok's Best Department Store
There are a number of department stores in the city but Central Chit Lom is number one – the place to visit for quality merchandise at fixed prices. There are seven storeys, packed with people every day between 9 am and 10 at night, and you will need plenty of stamina if indulging in some long-haul shopping. Luckily, there is a superb food centre on the premises, Food Loft. The next best to Central in terms of quality and price is Robinson's on Sukhumvit Road (see page 71).
✉ Phloenchit Rd
☎ 026 557 777
🚇 Chit Lom (Skytrain)

Charoennakorn Rd, Klongsan
✉ The Sheraton Grande Sukhumvit, 250 Sukhumvit Rd (see page 57)
✉ Amari Watergate Hotel, 847 Petchaburi Rd, Pratunam
✉ The Oriental Hotel, Oriental Avenue
✉ The Emporium, Sukhumvit Rd (see page 71)
✉ Central Chitlom, Phloenchit Rd

Narai Phand

This large craft centre is near the corner by the Gaysorn Plaza shopping mall; look for the street entrance nearby. Inside there are three levels packed with arts and crafts of every description, all with fixed prices, including silk and other fabrics.
✉ 127 Ratchadamri Avenue, corner of Ratchadamri Road and Phloenchit Road
☎ 022 524 670
🚇 Chit Lom
🖥 www.naraiphand.com

Silom Village

The main centre for shopping along Silom Road (see page 39), incorporating the **Ruen Thep Thai dance show** (see page 73), is a complex of individual shops retailing arts and crafts, souvenirs and luggage. Aimed squarely at visitors, there is a danger of being fleeced if you don't have a good idea of the value of the merchandise.
✉ 286 Silom Rd
☎ 026 357 523
🚇 Surasak or
🚢 Central Pier or Oriental Pier
🖥 www.silomvillage.co.th

Suan Lum Night Bazaar

This relatively new shopping venue wins hands down for accessibility, comfort, atmosphere and value for money. Here you will find the largest concentration of arts and crafts shops in the city, and far better value than most of the shops along

Silom Road or in River City. The bazaar is constituted by mostly individual, small-scale enterprises who have sourced interesting and eclectic craft and home decoration items. The market is not oppressively packed like Chatuchak and you do not have to engage in lengthy bargaining sessions to secure a reasonable price. Most of what is for sale has a marked price that is rarely outrageous and some gentle negotiation will usually secure a discount of 10–15%.

✉ Rama IV Rd

M Lumphini or

🚇 Sala Daeng

Taekee Taekon

If walking from the pier to Khao San Road along Phra Athit Road, you will pass this neat little shop of quality crafts. Prices are not outrageous, taking into account a small discount that will be yours for the asking.

✉ 118 Phra Athit Rd

☎ 026 291 473

🚉 Tha Phra Athit

🕐 until 18:00, closed Sunday.

Beauty Products
Go With the Flow

Skin-care products positioned at the quality end of the beauty products market – hence the up market locations of the distribution chain – nicely packaged and priced accordingly. Some of the ingredients are intriguing, like the body lotion made from chamomile and patchouli, with a dash of peppermint and geranium.

✉ Four Seasons Hotel, 155 Rajdamri Rd (see page 59)

✉ Shambhala Health Club & Spa, Metropolitan Hotel, 27 South Sathorn Rd (see page 60)

✉ Senada Theory, Gaysorn Plaza, Ploen Chit Rd (see page 52)

💻 go-with-the-flow.com

Below: Nearly all the malls have dedicated food centres.

Sukhumvit Rd

The largest concentration of shops, street stalls, department stores and shopping malls is to be found along Sukhumvit Road and its numerous *sois*. **Robinson's** department store and the **Times Square** shopping mall are both on the main road between Sois 17 and 19 and a little further down, heading east away from the city centre, is the **Emporium** mall. The other end of Sukhumvit Road, served by Skytrain's Nana and Asok stations, is packed with a variety of small shops where your bargaining skills are required and the pavements are packed with stalls selling a little bit of everything.

Quality Control
The range of arts and crafts on sale in Bangkok is dazzling but there are huge differences in quality – and price is not always a reliable guide. It is probably sensible to avoid buying a very expensive item, especially in the field of jewellery and antiques, unless you feel confident in judging the quality of the merchandise.

Central Drug
✉ *Top's Supermarket, Central Chidlom*

Nandakwang
✉ *Sukhumvit 23;*
✉ *Siam Discovery*

Sasivara Health and Beauty Center
✉ *Sukhumvit 39*

Villa Supermarket
✉ *J Avenue;*
✉ *Sukhumvit 49;*
✉ *Sukhumvit 33;*
✉ *Ploenchit;*
✉ *Lang Suan;*
✉ *Silom;*
✉ *Paholyothin;*
✉ *Nichada Thanee.*

Harnn Natural Home Spa
An Asian company, now worldwide, with an attractive range of products using natural ingredients. These stores are the place to linger for a choice of soaps and other items for the bathroom and the home.
✉ *Exotic Thai, 4th Floor, The Emporium, Sukhumvit Rd,*
☎ *026 648 000;*
✉ *Central Chitlom ,*
5th Floor, Ploenchit Rd.,
☎ *026 557 777;*
✉ *Design Sanctuary, 3rd Floor, Gaysorn Plaza* (see page 53)
✉ *Ploenchit Rd*
☎ *026 561 149;*
✉ *Siam Discovery Center, 4th Floor, Rama I Rd.*
☎ *026 581 000,*
🖥 *www.harnn. com*

Hombre
Quality skincare products for men which, like Go With The Flow (above), are only available at selected spas. Natural ingredients, especially grape skin and grapeseed extract, and nothing tested on animals.
✉ *Four Seasons Hotel, 155 Rajdamri Rd (see page 59);*
✉ *Shambhala Health Club & Spa, Metropolitan Hotel, 27 South Sathorn Rd (see page 60);*
✉ *Senada Theory, Gaysorn Plaza, Ploen Chit Rd (see page 53)*

⌨ *www.hombre*
formen.com

Shopping Malls

Emporium

Fairly typical of the city's plush shopping malls, the Emporium is noteworthy because it manages to pack some variety into its outlets and, unlike some, is not an endless stream of familiar, expensive brand names (though they are here as well). Quality silk at a Jim Thompson shop (*see* page 49), more than one bookshop, a good pharmacy and a rather superior supermarket.

✉ *Sukhumvit Rd (between Soi 22 and 24)*
☎ *022 890 235*
🚇 *Phrom Phong*
🕓 *Little is open before 10:00; closing time is 20:00.*

Gaysorn Plaza

Arriving by Skytrain, look for the pedestrian walkway from the station that leads you into this temple of high-class consumerism. Once safely cocooned inside, have your credit cards ready for some serious brand-name shopping. What you see is what you get – Prada, Dior, Louis Vuitton, Gucci - and no shoddy imitations or factory seconds. If the prices prove alarming, consider a dive into Patpong street market (*see* page 24) where ersatz versions of the handbags and wallets are readily available.

✉ *Phloenchit Rd*
☎ *026 559 561*
🚇 *Chit Lom*

MBK

No shopping trip to Bangkok is complete without a visit to the vast MBK shopping centre, especially if you are looking for clothes and shoes. Some of the shops have fixed prices, usually clearly displayed, but just as many are open to negotiation and where no price is on show you need to have a good idea of what the item is worth. A visit can be exhausting and it is best to avoid weekends unless you enjoy feeling like a sardine in a can.

✉ *junction of Phayathai Rd and Rama I Rd*
☎ *022 179 111*
🚇 *National Stadium*

Panthip

Only come here if you are interested in computer software and hardware or CDs and DVDs of music and movies. If you are tempted by the pirated material, be prepared to feel like a criminal as you wait with your ticket number for the illegal goods to arrive. The atmosphere is oppressive and male and there is nowhere decent to enjoy a drink or meal.

✉ *Petchaburi Rd*
☎ *026 458 921*
🚇 *Ratchatewi*

WHERE TO STAY

It is worth considering the location of your planned accommodation so as to minimize time spent travelling across the city and this is especially true if you intend to spend a lot of time in one activity. It makes sense to book somewhere in the Sukhumvit Road area if you want to do a lot of shopping and while there are quite a few five-star hotels in Sukhumvit there are also a number of smart mid-range places to stay. Sukhumvit also has the advantage of being served by the Skytrain and Metro and there is a healthy nightlife with lots of restaurants and bars open until late.

The number of hotels and guesthouses around Siam Square is smaller but equally central and well connected to the city's transport links. There is a concentration of mid-range places on Soi Kasemsan 1 and luxury hotels are also in the vicinity.

If temples and cultural pursuits are the order of the day, and if you want to get away from glitzy hotels, then the Khao San Road area beckons. Traditionally, this is the budget traveller's territory but in the last few years a number of mid-range hotels and guesthouses

Below: *All the top hotels have plush interiors and a choice of eating venues.*

have sprung up offering comfortable rooms, amenities and security. A drawback for some visitors in this area is the lack of Skytrain or Metro transport, although you can get around using river and canal boats.

Chinatown has atmosphere but limited accommodation and while the Grand China Princess suggests itself as the best place to stay there are some other options. It is not the best area for ease of transport and you will find yourself using taxis and the river boat service.

How to Book

Having settled on a location and a budget, the best way to book a room is online using either the hotel's website or one of the countless accommodation agencies. Room rates are competitive and special deals from the chain hotels are always worth looking out for. It is also worth checking any deals that might be available through the airline you use. The room rates given here are always the official rack rates and with the more expensive establishments you should expect a sizeable discount on the web. For many of the mid-range and budget hotels, where prices are economical to begin with, expect less of a discount.

Hotel Facilities

Unless otherwise stated, all the hotels listed have rooms with airconditioning, television and telephone; and room rates include a buffet breakfast. Luxury hotels will have all the trimmings. Most places will have internet access, although sometimes the rates for guests are high. It is not only five-star hotels that have a left luggage facility so always ask if you are planning an excursion.

Accommodation websites
www. siam.net/tiger
www.khaosan road.com
www.airasia.com
www.hostels.com
www.hostelworld.com

Hotels Worth Considering
Sukhumvit Road Area, *budget to mid-range*: **Suk 11 and The Atlanta** (*see* page 56) *Luxury*: **Sheraton Grande Sukhumvit** (*see* page 57)

Khao San Road Area, *budget to mid-range*: **Buddy Lodge** (*see* page 58)

Chinatown, *mid-range*: **Grand China Princess** (*see* page 59)

Silom Road Area, *budget*: **Sathorn Inn** (*see* page 60)

Sukhumvit Road Area

• *BUDGET*

Premier Travelodge
(Map B–I5)
Functional but inexpensive accommodation in a location where most visitors are paying a lot more for their bedrooms. There is no restaurant, hence no breakfast, but this is not a problem around Sukhumvit. There are just under 50 rooms, each with a safety deposit box, telephone and fridge. ⊠ *170, Soi 8, Sukhumvit Rd,* ☎ *022 251 3031, Room rates: B700 (excluding breakfast),* 🕭 *Nana*

Suk 11 (Map B–I5)
All 60 beds are often booked so plan a stay here in advance, especially if you want one of the en-suite rooms. Others share bathroom facilities, as do the dorm beds. The décor and rural style makes Suk 11 one of the more enchanting places to stay anywhere in the city, a veritable oasis of peace and calm amidst the urban mayhem. ⊠ *1/33 Sukhumvit Soi 11,* ☎ *022 535 929,* 🖳 *www.suk11.com Room rates: B250– B700,* 🕭 *Nana*

• *MID-RANGE*

The Atlanta
(Map B–I5)
Probably the most interesting and characterful hotel in Bangkok and worth the hassle of having to book a room without the convenience of the Internet, and one that doesn't accept credit cards. The Atlanta has changed little in many decades and seems determined to keep the décor and ambience stuck firmly in the past. The foyer dates back to the 1950s, with a style modelled on theatre set designs of the 1930s, and has the distinction of being the most filmed and photographed foyer in Thailand. Of the 70 rooms, the best value ones are those with airconditioning. There are two pools, a restaurant and a travel information desk. At the bottom end of Soi 2 in a quiet location, the hectic delights of Sukhumvit are a short walk away. ⊠ *78 Soi 2, Sukhumvit Rd,* ☎ *022 526 069,* 📠 *026 568 123,* 🖳 *www.theatlanta hotel.bizland.com Room rates: B330– B1300,* 🕭 *Nana*

City Lodge
(Map B–I4)
Two neat little hotels, with under 30 rooms in Soi 9 and 40 in Soi 19, which offer good value for money. Service and facilities are fairly good for this price range, with room service from early morning until 22:00 and a mini-bar in each room, plus free use of the pool and gym in the nearby Amari Boulevard Hotel. City Lodge in Soi 9 has a pleasant informal restaurant while Soi 19 has an Italian restaurant, both open all day. ⊠ *Soi 9 and Soi 19, Sukhumvit Rd,* ☎ *022 537 705 (Soi 9); 022 544*

783 (Soi 19), 🖳 *www.amari.com   Room rates: B1520–B2000,* 🚇 *Nana*

• LUXURY

Imperial Queen's Park Hotel

(Map B–I5)

One of the largest hotels in the city, with over 1300 rooms in two 37-storey towers. The staff may not get to know you by name but in return for the anonymity there are seven restaurants, bar, swimming pool, health and spa facilities and an air of luxury about the place.

✉ *Soi 22, Sukhumvit Rd,* ☎ *022 619 000,* 🖳 *www.imperialhotels.com   Room rates: from B7600,* 🚇 *Phrom Phong*

JW Marriott

(Map B–I5)

A well-known hotel on Sukhumvit Road that manages to work equally well with business and non-business guests. There is a choice of rooms, all with broadband connection, spa, pool, 24-hour gym, courteous and knowledgeable service, superb restaurants and bars. Alongside the signature steakhouse, there is a Thai and a Chinese restaurant and a bar on street level that is a popular meeting place for city residents.

✉ *Soi 2, Sukhumvit Rd* ☎ *026 567 700,* 🖳 *www.marriott.com/bkkdt   Room rates: from B8500* 🚇 *Nana*

Majestic Grande

(Map B–I5)

A relatively new hotel that opened a couple of years ago and still benefits from that brand new feeling. The official room rates put it firmly into the luxury category but, at the time of writing, there were discounted rates on the standard bedrooms that pushed the rate below B5000. The location is a quiet one, with all the action just a short walk away, and there is a pool and restaurant.

✉ *12 Soi 2, Sukhumvit Rd,* ☎ *022 622 999,* 🖳 *www.majesticgrande.com   Room rates: from B5000* 🚇 *Nana*

Sheraton Grande Sukhumvit

(Map B–I5)

The most luxurious accommodation on Sukhumvit Road, and can hold its own with any of the many five-star hotels in Bangkok. Bedrooms are larger than average and come with all the amenities. Two excellent restaurants, live music in the bar and a gregarious atmosphere. Over 400 rooms in a tower block of 33 storeys.

✉ *250 Sukhumvit Rd* ☎ *026 498 888,* 🖳 *www.starwoodhotels.com/bangkok   Room rates: B7000* 🚇 *Asok*

Khao San Road Area

• BUDGET

Thai Cozy House

(Map B–B2)

Budget accommodation close to Khao San

Road that seeks to maintain basic standards of cleanliness and service. The best rooms have a window so don't expect too much from the least expensive ones. Breakfast only comes with the better rooms as well, though this is hardly a problem in this neighbourhood. ⊠ 113/1-3 Tanee Rd ☎ 026 295 870, 🖳 www.thaicozy house.com Room rates: B700–B850, 🚇 Tha Praya Athit

• MID-RANGE
Buddy Lodge
(Map B–B3)
This hotel reflects the new side of Khao San Road, offering over 40 clean and comfortable bedrooms with safe deposit boxes and professional service. There is a small pool, for lounging by the side of rather than swimming in, and a useful travel desk. A small café is on the premises but the neighbourhood heaves with restaurants. ⊠ 265 Khao San Rd ☎ 026 294 477, 🖳 www.buddylodge. com Room rates: B1800–B2200, 🚇 Tha Praya Athit

Viengtai Hotel
(Map B–B2)
A 200-room, well-managed hotel in the heart of the Khao San Road neighbourhood. Comfortable rooms and a restaurant open throughout the day. Along with Buddy Lodge, the best place to stay in this corner of the city. ⊠ 42 Rambuttri Rd ☎ 028 181 153, 🖳 www.viengtai.co.th Room rates: B1750-B2350, 🚇 Tha Praya Athit

Chinatown Area
• BUDGET
Krung Kasem Sri Krung Hotel
(Map B–D5)
A useful 50-room hotel to know about if you arrive late in the city by train or have an early departure and just want a cheap place to sleep for a night. The bedrooms are clean and the beds are comfortable, there is a laundry service and a café. From the main railway entrance, outside the Metro station, look to your right and cross the bridge over the canal. Krung Kasem Road is on the right at the traffic lights and the hotel sign is visible from here. ⊠ 1860 Krung Kasem Rd, ☎ 022 250 132 Room rates: B560, M Hua Lamphong

• MID-RANGE
The Chinatown Hotel (Map B–D5)
A recently renovated hotel that now offers comfortable accommodation with room amenities including safe deposit box and mini bar. Room rates are reasonable, and although the location is perhaps not ideal for a long stay, the neighbourhood is close to the railway station. There are 75 rooms. ⊠ 526 Yaowarat Rd

☎ 022 502 326,
🖥 www.chinatown hotel.co.th   Room rates: B950–B1200
Ⓜ Hua Lamphong

Grand China Princess (Map B–C4)

Easily the best hotel in Chinatown, a gregarious establishment with good facilities by way of places to eat – a café on the second floor, daily lunch buffet and a revolving restaurant at the top of the building. A swimming pool, fitness centre and massage service. Over 150 rooms.
✉ 27 Yaowarat Rd
☎ 022 249 977,
🖥 www.grandchina. com   Room rates: B2600–B4700,
Ⓜ Hua Lamphong

Siam Square & World Plaza Area

• *BUDGET*

Reno Hotel
(Map B–F4)

Soi Kasemson 1 has quite a few places to stay but some are better than others and the

Reno comes out on top. The management make an effort to present an attractive establishment with visitor-oriented facilities: Internet in the lobby, a small pool, laundry service, travel desk, a café. All 52 bedrooms have a safe deposit box and the larger rooms have their own fridge.
✉ 40 Soi Kasemson 1, off Rama I Rd, ☎ 022 150 026, 🖥 renohotel@ dickta.com Room rates: B870–B1180, 🚇 Siam

• *LUXURY*
The Four Seasons
(Map B–H5)

A superb establishment where all 340 rooms deliver comfort and luxury. Thai furniture, modern and antique, and Jim Thompson silks contribute to the air of refined elegance that characterizes the hotel. All the amenities and services, including an executive club, business centre, concierge services, quality restaurants, health club, spa and pool. One of the best hotels in the city.

✉ 155 Rajadamri Rd
☎ 022 501 000,
🖥 www.fourseasons. com   Room rates: from B5500, 🚇 Chit Lom

Novotel Bangkok
(Map B–G4)

If you want to be close to the shops and feel the buzz of central Bangkok, but aren't too fussed over the interior design of your hotel, then the Novotel (or the Pathumwan Princess below) fits the bill. The foyer is usually heaving with people – functions are always taking place – the restaurants are busy and the nightclub keeps the place busy at night.
✉ Soi 6, Siam Square
☎ 022 556 888,
🖥 www.accorhotels. com/asia   Room rates: from B5500, 🚇 Siam

Pathumwan Princess (Map B–F4)

Not the most charming of hotels but if you want a short run from shopping malls like the MBK Centre (see page 52) then this is the most convenient place to stay. There are over 450 rooms, all comfortably furnished and maintained, and a swimming pool, spa, tennis and squash courts.

✉ *444 Phaya Thai Rd*
☎ *022 163 700,*
🖥 *www.princess.com*
Room rates: from B5600, 🚇 *National Stadium*

Silom Road Area

• *BUDGET*
Sathon Inn

(Map C–E6)

Accommodation around Silom Road is usually more expensive than this but people who stay at the Sathorn Inn like the place. The 30 rooms come in different sizes and the better ones have their own fridge. There is a café on the premises, though breakfast is extra.

✉ *27 Sathon Tai Rd*
☎ *022 381 655,* 📠 *022 376 668,* ✉ *sathorninn @hotmail.com Room rates: B900–B1500,*

excluding breakfast
🚇 *Chong Nonsi*

• *MID-RANGE*
The Swiss Lodge

(Map B–G6)

Typical of the city's better quality accommodation that doesn't come in the form of a skyscraper hotel. But you still get 24-hr room service, smart bedrooms furnished in a contemporary style, easy on the eye, plus attentive service.

✉ *3 Convent Rd*
☎ *022 335 345,*
🖥 *www.swisslodge. com Room rates: B4,900–B5,300,*
🚇 *Sala Daeng*

• *LUXURY*
The Metropolitan

(Map C–H6)

One of the most chic hotels in the city, The Metropolitan attracts the arty and elegant who value the virtues of fashion. The stylish interior emphases clarity, light and good living and this is reflected in the menus of the two restaurants, the **Cyan** and the

informal **Glow**, and the oh-so-cool **Met Bar**. There is a swimming pool, of course, and a sophisticated spa, the Shambhala, where guests benefit from a free 15-minute massage of the head and shoulders.

✉ *27 Sathon Tai Rd*
☎ *026 253 333,*
🖥 *www.metro politan.como.bz Room rates: from B5000,* 🚇 *Nana*

Chao Phraya River

• *LUXURY*
The Oriental

(Map C–A4)

A famous hotel, once the haunt of celebrities and still a name to conjure with while cashing in on an illustrious history. The Oriental makes the best of its site (which includes a section on the other bank of the river) to cram in nearly 400 rooms, a pool, gym, spa, tennis courts and expensive restaurants.

✉ *48 Oriental Avenue*
☎ *026 599 000,*

🖥 www.mandarin. com   Room rates: from B13,200, 🚤 Saphan Taksin, 🚇 Oriental

The Peninsula

(Map B–C6)

The Peninsula is special, not least because it is situated on the west bank of the Chao Phraya River and, with a shuttle boat running on demand, the location presents no practical problem. The hotel itself is superb and outclasses The Oriental in most respects. To enjoy the spectacular views at maximum intensity, reserve one of the 370 rooms that are above the first few storeys.

✉ 333 Charoennakorn, Klongsan Rd

☎ 028 612 888,

🖥 www.peninsula. com   Room rates: from B7600

Shangri-La Hotel

(Map C–A5)

A landmark hotel that has established itself as one of the best places to stay in Bangkok. It is a split-site hotel, connected by corridors

and a motorized buggy, and everywhere the service and facilities are top-drawer: superb restaurants, spa, pools, gym. Nearly 800 rooms.

✉ 89 Soi Wat Suan Plu, ☎ 022 367 777, 🖥 www.shangri-la.com Room rates: from B5500, 🚤 Saphan Taksin, 🚇 Central pier

Other Areas

Nai Lert Park

(Map B–H4)

If you came to Bangkok years ago and stayed in the Hilton, you will be astonished at the changes that have been made to this hotel. The Nai Lert Park is a charming

place to stay, not least because of the extensive gardens where you can escape from the urban jungle and relax in the shade of tropical vegetation or by the pool. The style of the hotel is contemporary and engaging with three very good restaurants – and Central Chidlom (see page 51) is a short walk away through the back exit.

✉ 2 Withayu Rd,

☎ 022 530 123,

🖥 www.nailerpark. swisshotel.com   Room rates: from B4500,

🚤 Phloen Chit

Below: The Shangri-La hotel complex on the east side of the Chao Phraya River.

EATING OUT
Where to Eat

You will never be away from food in Bangkok and the only difficulty rests with the burden of choice. Even in places where a menu in English is not available, it is only a matter of pointing to something that takes your fancy; if you like **Thai food** you are unlikely to be disappointed by what appears on your plate.

If you want to play safe and stick to restaurants where non-Thai visitors and menus in English are common – and where, therefore, spices are used with a degree of restraint – the Sukhumvit Road area is probably your best bet. Here, there is a multiplicity of establishments serving **Western** junk food, **Asian** fast-food, formal and informal **Thai** eateries, **Indian** restaurants and the whole mouth-watering gamut of **Asian cuisine**.

Informal and frequent eating is intrinsic to Thai culture and you are never far from a food centre, informal eatery or street stall cooking fresh and delicious dishes before your eyes. For a formal meal at night, some of the best restaurants are to be found in hotels and it is here where foreign chefs experienced in European, Chinese, Thai, and Japanese cooking excel.

The competition between hotel restaurants is such that many new dishes and even whole menus are concocted afresh on a regular basis.

Below: *Tasty food is available at a variety of outdoor establishments, like this seafood restaurant in Chinatown.*

Eating on the Hoof

Central Bangkok fills with millions of workers every day and they all need feeding quickly, efficiently and inexpensively, and if you want a quick but tasty meal that comes on a plate and not in a polystyrene box it is simply a matter of joining them in the **food centres** and **street stalls** that are everywhere. Most of the large shopping plazas, like the MBK Centre and those along Sukhumvit Road, have one storey (usually at the very top or in the basement) given over to a food centre. Packed with office workers from breakfast time onwards, their menus are often but not always in English and you can usually see the ingredients being cooked.

As an example of how a food centre can evolve into something quite sophisticated, check out the Food Loft in Central Chidlom (*see* page 68).

Paying the Bill

In formal restaurants you will be presented with a bill, including any service charge, and payment can be made in cash or with a credit card. In informal eateries, you may be able to work out the cost from a menu but sometimes it is a matter of just paying the amount requested, either before or after you eat. You are highly unlikely to

Above: *A food stall at a night market.*

Dining by the Chao Phraya River

No, not a cruise with a buffet where you queue up for pre-cooked food. Supatra River House is a converted house by the river offering atmospheric views and reasonable Thai food which is never too hot to handle.
✉ 226 Soi Wat-Rakang
☎ 024 110 305 (or 024 110 874)
The easiest way to get there is by the special Supatra ferry from the Tha Maharaj pier
🕙 11:00–14:00 for lunch and 17:30–22:30 at night.

ever be cheated and, anyway, many food vendors know enough English to make clear their charge.

In many food centres, a coupon system operates: purchase coupons at the kiosk and use these to pay the individual food stalls, then return to the kiosk for a refund of unused ones.

Healthy Eating

Health-conscious eateries are all the rage in Bangkok and as well as restaurants such as **Glow** and **Amaranth**, the following are also worth knowing about:

The Third Floor

The theory behind the menu at this restaurant is that different blood groups benefit from different diets so you need to know your own blood group when choosing your dishes. ✉ 3/F, Versau Building, Wireless Rd, ☎ 022 548 101, 🕐 10:30–19:00 daily.

Whole Earth

There are low tables and casual dining downstairs, and a more formal arrangement upstairs. The menu has lots of vegetarian choices but also offers white meat and fish dishes; no red meat. ✉ 71 Soi 26, Sukhumvit Rd, ☎ 022 584 900, 🕐 11:30–14:00; 17:30–22:30 daily.

Rasayana

Raw food is the main draw at Rasayana, and all the ingredients are washed in purified water to maximize bodily health. ✉ Soi 39, Sukhumvit Rd, ☎ 026 624 803, 🕐 10:00–20:00 daily.

West Side of the River
Mei Jiang
Chinese cuisine at its most elegant and refined, a trip to Mei Jiang is well worth travelling across the Chao Phraya River on the hotel's free shuttle boat. The range of Chinese teas is delightful and the food delectable. ✉ Peninsula Hotel, 333 Charoen Nakorn Rd, ☎ 028 612 888, 🕐 11:30–14:30, 18:00–22:30 daily, 🚢 The Peninsula pier, next to Central Pier

Jester's
If Chinese food is not what you're after then still make the trip to the Peninsula and head for Jester's. Fusion food of the highest order and it can almost be guaranteed that you will not leave disappointed. ✉ Peninsula Hotel, 333 Charoen Nakorn Rd, ☎ 028 612 888, 🕐 11:30–14:30, 18:00–22:30 daily, 🚢 The Peninsula pier, next to Central Pier

Sukhumvit Road Area

• *LUXURY*
A Garden

Brunch, lunch, afternoon tea (Fri–Sat 14:00–18:00) and dinner in salubrious surroundings where you choose between an air-conditioned dining room or a lovely shady garden. French and Italian cuisine; delicacies like foie gras.

✉ 64, Soi 51
Sukhumvit Rd
☎ 022 604 992
🕐 10:00–23:00 daily
🚇 Thong Lo

Les Nymphéas

French food without the heavy sauces and obsession with red meat; having said that, the steak is a favourite with many. The décor is startling – check out the Monet reproductions – and the cooking is creative.

✉ 4/F, Imperial Queen's Park Hotel, Soi 22, 109 Sukhumvit Rd, ☎ 026 619 300, 🕐 11:30–14:30, 18:30–22:30
🚇 Phrom Phong

Lyon

French food at its best and an atmosphere to match. All is peaceful, with soft lighting and subdued white décor. Reservations are essential. A good bar, wine list (you can dine downstairs in the cellar), and the *coq au vin* is a winner.

✉ 33/2 Ruam Rudee, Soi 2, ☎ 022 538 141, 🕐 11:30–14:00, 18:30–22.30 daily, 🚇 Ploenchit

Red Pepper

A well-established Thai restaurant serving quality Thai dishes in congenial surroundings; reserve a table by the window looking out on the garden. Live music most nights, easy-going atmosphere.

✉ G/F, Rembrandt, 19 Soi, 18 Sukhumvit Rd ☎ 022 617 100, 🕐 17:00–23:00 daily, 🚇 Phrom Phong

White Elephant

If you are new to Thai food and worried about too much chili but want to sample a bit of everything – or if you just want to eat a lot of Thai food – the buffet is recommended.
✉ JW Marriott Hotel, Soi 2, Sukhumvit Rd, ☎ 022 553 767, 🕐 11:30–14:30 and 18:30–22:30 daily, 🚇 Chit Lom

• *MID-RANGE*
Amaranth

The menu at this health-conscious eatery includes information on the calories and nutritional content of each dish. The purist décor adds to the feeling of eating what is good for you. Fusion-style dishes, like Cajun-style papaya with fish, plus juices, smoothies and wine (organic of course).
✉ 545 Soi 31, Sukhumvit Rd, ☎ 026 620 795, 🕐 11:30–14:30; 18:00–22:00 daily, 🚇 Phrom Phong

Himali Cha Cha & Son

A restaurant with a reputation for excellent Indian food and an interesting history associated with the

man, 'Uncle Himali', who settled in Bangkok after serving as cook to Lord Mountbatten when he was British Viceroy in India. There is a branch at 1229/11 Charoen Krung Rd.
✉ 2, Soi 35, Sukhumvit Rd, ☎ 022 588 843, ⏰ 11:30–15:30, 18:00–22:30 daily, 🚇 Phrom Phong

Nipa Thai

Thai dishes as authentic as you request in terms of spices and chilis – be warned! All the favourites are here, including tom yam soup, and the lemon grass and ginger ice-cream is a treat. Live music at night. A good meal will cost around B600; less at lunchtime.
✉ The Landmark, 138 Sukhumvit Rd, ☎ 022 540 404, ext. 4305, 🖥 www.landmark bangkok.com ⏰ 11:30–14:30, 18:00–22:30 daily, 🚇 Nana

Seafood Town

If you are a seafood aficionado, the choice of live seafood – see

for yourself in the tanks – is exemplary. The desserts are recommended but take a long time to arrive.
✉ 7, Soi 24 Sukhumvit Rd, ☎ 026 610 037, ⏰ 11:00–14:00, 17:00–22:00 daily, 🚇 Nana

• BUDGET
Dosa King

For a tasty, inexpensive Indian vegetarian meal, Dosa King is an ideal choice. It is easy to find – clearly visible on Sukhumvit Road and close to the corner with Soi 19 – and a meal can be enjoyed for under B400.
✉ 265/1 Soi 19, Sukhumvit Rd, ☎ 026 651 651, ⏰ 11:00–23:00 daily, 🚇 Nana

Govinda

Vegetarian again but this time Italian, with the bonus of a restful outdoor dining area (where smoking is allowed). Pizzas are a speciality; also pasta dishes plus home-made ice cream and bread. A reservation is useful, especially at weekends.

✉ 6566, Soi 22, Sukhumvit Rd, ☎ 026 634 970, ⏰ Wed–Mon, 11:30–15:00; 18:00 to midnight, 🚇 Nana

Lemon Grass

Lemon grass is fairly essential in Thai and Southeast Asian cooking and you will appreciate its value as an ingredient after sampling some of the delicious dishes in this attractive little townhouse restaurant.
✉ 5/1 Soi 24, Sukhumvit Rd, ☎ 022 588 637, ⏰ 11:00–14:00, 18:00–23:00 daily, 🚇 Phrom Phong

Tamarind Café

A trendy, three-storey restaurant filled with photographs and comfortable sofas. The menu is a vegetarian one, with an emphasis on health, but there are also some delicious, weight-gaining cakes to round off a meal.
✉ 27, Soi 20, Sukhumvit Rd, ☎ 026 637 421, ⏰ Wed–Fri, 11:00–23:00; Sat–Sun 09:00–23:00, 🚇 Nana

Siam Square and World Trade Centre Area

• LUXURY

Aubege Dab

A fine place for an evening meal if you need a break from Asian food. Exquisite French cuisine, wood-panelled décor and pristine tableware. Soft, live music adds to the mood and the menu offers duck liver and other French favourites.

✉ 1st Level, Mercury Tower, 540 Ploenchit Rd, ☎ 026 586 222, ⏱ 11:30–14:30, 18:30–22:30 daily, 🚇 Chit Lom

Biscotti

Popular with residents of the city who appreciate reliably good food, a cool ambience and a decent Italian wine list (starting at B1450 a bottle). The menu regularly changes. Obviously a pizza will cost less than a steak, but expect to pay around B1000 for a three-course meal at night.

✉ Four Seasons Hotel, 155 Rajdamri Rd, ☎ 022 501 000, ⏱ 11:30–14:30, 18:30–22:30 daily, 🚇 Chit Lom

C'Est Bon

It is good, the food that is; the setting is less so, looking out across a grim parking lot. The food is French and Vietnamese and the set menu is the best value for money in terms of experiencing some new tastes.

✉ G/F, International Hotel, 975 Ploenchit Rd, ☎ 026 561 531, ⏱ 17:30 to midnight daily, 🚇 Chit Lom

• MID-RANGE

Baan Khanitha

If you want quality Thai food but without shocking your tastebuds, this fits the bill. It is like the White Elephant (*see page* 65) in this respect but instead of a hotel setting the context is a modern Thai house reflecting traditional art and design. Reservations are useful at weekends.

✉ 49 Soi Ruam Rudee, ☎ 022 534 638, ⏱ 11:00–14:00, 18:00–23:00 daily, 🚇 Ploenchit

Senses

Suits the style of this up-market shopping mall. The food is thoroughly fusion and suitable for a repast before heading off once more on the consumer trail.

✉ 1/F Gaysorn Plaza, ☎ 026 071, ⏱ 10:00–21:00 daily, 🚇 Chit Lom

Liu

Imagine what a fancy Chinese restaurant looked like in 1930s Shanghai, complete with live, classical Chinese music, and this is it. Dim sum is the main draw at lunchtime while evening offers an extensive menu.

✉ 3/F, Conrad Hotel, Wireless Rd, ☎ 026 909 255, ⏱ Mon–Sat 11:30–14:00, 18:00–23:00; Sun 10:30–14:00, 18:00–23:00, 🚇 Ploenchit

Nippon Tei

Well-known to regular visitors and expatriates as a place to enjoy authentic Japanese dishes. Sashimi, sushi, Kobe beef, seafood in a classic setting of white wood and Japanese screens. ✉ *Basement, Thai Obayashi Building, 161 Rajdamri Rd,* ☎ *022 529 438,* ⏰ *11:00–14:00, 17:00–22:00 daily,* 🚇 *Rajdamri*

Outback Steakhouse

A grill house with an Australian theme and, till US beef is allowed back into the country, Australian sourced as well. Steaks are big, prices reasonable. ✉ *2/F, Siam Discovery Centre,* ☎ *026 580 202,* ⏰ *11:30–22:30 daily,* 🚇 *Siam*

• *BUDGET*
Food Loft

After shopping in the Central Chidlom department store you will need rest and recuperation, and the Food Loft is at hand to provide it. Chinese, Thai, Japanese, Italian, Vietnamese, Korean and Malaysian food – mix and match to taste. A good meal will be under B300. ✉ *7th Level, Central Chidlom, Ploenchit Rd,* ☎ *026 557 777,* ⏰ *09:00–22:00 daily,* 🚇 *Chit Lom*

Gallery Eleven

This eatery is tucked away to the side of Soi 11, but the Ambassador Hotel across the street is a useful marker. There is no air conditioning but the character of the place more than compensates. Inexpensive Thai food, expect to pay around B300 for three courses, and a range of alcoholic drinks. ✉ *Sukhumvit Soi 11,* ☎ *026 512 672,* ⏰ *09:00–23:00 daily,* 🚇 *Nana*

Holy Pizza

Not sure what's holy about the pizzas here but they are delicious and served quickly, just what you need after a shopping trip around Siam Square. ✉ *442 Siam Square, Soi 7,* ☎ *026 546 373,* ⏰ *11:00–23:00 daily,* 🚇 *Siam*

Hong Kong Noodle

Worth knowing about when you are whacked from shopping and want to escape from the scene. The menu has pictures so you know what your dish is going to look like and rest assured it will be tasty. Good value. ✉ *430 Siam Square, Soi 10,* ☎ *022 548 755* ⏰ *10:00–22:00 daily,* 🚇 *Siam*

Vanilla Industry

The name is not a clue to the food or the ambience as the food is mainly Italian with an international inflection. Downstairs is a take-away outlet for cakes and other goodies; go upstairs for the restaurant. ✉ *422 Siam Square, Soi 11,* ☎ *026 584 720* ⏰ *10:00–22:00 daily,* 🚇 *Siam*

Silom Road Area

• *LUXURY*

Celadon

Authentic Thai cuisine, including regional specialities, in a restaurant awarded Best Food in Thailand by a gourmet magazine in 2004. It has its own space surrounded by ponds. Set meals and à la carte provide a wide choice; expect to pay around B1000 for a dinner.
✉ *The Sukhothai, 13/3 South Sathon Rd,* ☎ *023 448 888,* 💻 *www.sukhothai. com* 🕐 *11:30–14:30, 18:30–22:30,* 🚤 *Sala Daeng,* **M** *Lumphini*

Glow

Mostly vegetarian and organic, the menu includes a satisfying burger with noodles, raw fish dishes and exotic salads. Wholesome fruit and vegetable drinks, plus organic spirits for those unworthy bodies still craving a gin or vodka.
✉ *The Metropolitan, 27 South Sathon Rd,* ☎ *026 253 366*
💻 *www.metro politan.como.bz* 🕐 *06:00–21:00 daily,* 🚤 *Nana,* **M** *Lumphini*

La Scala

Italian dishes delivered from an open kitchen suggest a gregarious restaurant but La Scala has a décor and design befitting more intimate meals. Top class food: buffet lunch around B800, dinner B1500.
✉ *The Sukhothai, 13/3 South Sathon Rd,* ☎ *023 448 888,* 💻 *www.sukhothai. com* 🕐 *11:30–14:30, 18:30–10:30,* 🚤 *Sala Daeng,* **M** *Lumphini*

Sirocco

The daft dress code won't allow sandals or shorts, but boots and torn jeans are OK. On the plus side, you are over 60 storeys high and eating al fresco – unparalleled views of the city at night. The Mediterranean food is nothing special considering the prices but then Sirocco's appeal is not to gourmets.

Also out in the open is the Sky Bar; even if not dining, have a drink here just to experience the situation. Live jazz music.
✉ *63rd level, State Tower, 1055 Silom Rd,* ☎ *026 249 555,* 🕐 *18:00–23:00 daily,* 🚤 *Saphan Taksin,* 🚢 *Central Pier or Oriental Pier*

Sorrento

For a romantic night out the setting – an old house tastefully converted into an atmospheric bistro – is restful and relaxing. The international food with an Italian bias is not especially wonderful, considering the prices.
✉ *66 Sathon Rd North,* ☎ *022 349 841,* 🕐 *11:00–14:00, 18:00–23:00 daily,* 🚤 *Surasak*

Vertigo

Competing with Sirocco for al fresco dining on top of the world. Mediterranean cuisine plus grills (the steak is recommended) and a romantic atmosphere. You won't find another like it anywhere in Thailand. ✉ *61st level, Banyan Tree Hotel, 21/100 South Sathon Rd*, ☎ *026 791 200*, 🖥 *www.banyantree.com*, ⏰ *18:30 to midnight daily*, 🚊 *Sala Daeng*, **M** *Lumphini*

• MID-RANGE
Café Di Roma

Quality Italian seafood. Expect to pay B450 to B700 for a three-course meal and a drink.
✉ *3 Patpong Soi 2*, ☎ *026 328 250*, ⏰ *18:00–02:00 daily*, 🚊 *Sala Daeng*

Le Bouchon

A great place to go after a trawl through Patpong (but see also Café di Roma above). Bistro-style French food, bring your own wine if you wish. Invigorating coffees.
✉ *37/17 Patpong Soi 2*, ☎ *022 349 109*, ⏰ *Mon–Sat, noon to 15:00, 18:00–23:30*, 🚊 *Sala Daeng*

Little India

Easy to find, opposite the Shangri-La hotel. The mouth-watering food is from the north of India. There's also a take-away service. Two people can expect to pay about B800.
✉ *64/38 Soi Wat Suan Plu*, ☎ *026 307 906*, ⏰ *11:00–23:00 daily*, 🚊 *Saphan Taksin*, 🚤 *Central Pier*

• BUDGET
Café de Laos

Thai-Lao food in a bright and elegant eatery worth seeking out for a light meal.
✉ *Soi 19, Silom Rd*, ☎ *026 352 338*, ⏰ *11:00–14:00, 17:00–22:00 daily*, 🚊 *Surasak*, 🚤 *Central Pier or Oriental Pier*

Jim Thompson's

Elegant setting with a lotus pond in a calm garden. The food is Thai but in a cosmopolitan way and there are Italian-style dishes as well. The desserts are a treat. Under B400 for one person, including a drink.

✉ *120 Saladaeng Soi 1, Silom Rd*, ☎ *022 669 167*, ⏰ *Sun–Thu, 11:00–21:30*, 🚊 *Sala Daeng*

Other Areas
Le Danang

Out of the city centre but worth a trip for the superb authentic Vietnamese food created by a female chef from Hanoi. Live music on a Friday night.
✉ *Sofitel Central Plaza, 1695 Phaholyothyhin Rd, Chatuchak*, ☎ *025 411 234, ext. 4041*, ⏰ *11:30–14:.30, 18:00–22:30 daily*, 🚊 *Mo Chit*, **M** *Chatuchak Park*

Keang Wang

This restaurant is not being recommended for its food but for its location – near the Grand Palace and on the left as you go towards the pier, on your right on the way to the palace. Basic chicken meals and one-plate dishes to satisfy hunger pangs.
✉ *77 Naphralan Rd*, ☎ *022 265 984*, ⏰ *11:00–21:00 daily*, 🚤 *Tha Chang pier*

ENTERTAINMENT
Nightlife

Bangkok is famous and also infamous for its nightlife, so there is quite a range of entertainment possibilities for the hours after dark. The *sois* off Sukhumvit Road are the main hunting ground for late-night revellers, but you will also find here some delightful little bars for just chilling out and taking it easy. Some of the best nightclubs in the city are also in the Sukhumvit Road area.

Another neighbourhood with a concentration of bars and clubs is Patpong and, although there are some places here well worth spending time in, there are also many sleazy joints catering mostly to sad men. Very nearby, Soi 4 off Silom Road has some excellent little bars and clubs.

Other nightspots are scattered around the metropolis but all are within a taxi ride of the city centre.

Cinemas

Cinemas are inexpensive (tickets cost between B70 and B150) but are nevertheless modern and comfortable and have excellent sound systems. Bangkok's cinemas are often situated on the top levels of shopping centres. The drawback is that only Hollywood releases tend to be shown with their original English soundtrack, with Thai subtitles. Whatever the film, audiences stand respectfully for the playing of the Thai national anthem before each performance. See ⌨ www.movieseer.com for current information about what's on.

Some cinemas in Bangkok can be found in the following locations: **Major Cineplex,**

Bars With a View

Moon Bar

The Moon Bar competes with the Sky Bar for that top-of-the-world experience and it is hard to beat for a pre- or post-dinner drink.
✉ 61/F Banyan Tree Hotel, 21/100 South Sathon Rd, ☎ 026 791 200, ⏰ daily 17:00–01:00 (weather permitting),
M Lumphini

Sky Bar

An open-air bar 250m (820ft) above the ground; you can come here for a cocktail any time and enjoy the stupendous views.
✉ 64th level, State Tower, 1055 Thanon Silom, ☎ 026 249 555, ⌨ www.the domebkk.com,
⏰ 18:30–01:00 daily,
🚤 Central Pier or Oriental Pier.
No sandals or shorts

Below: *Patpong pubs cater largely to visitors.*

Above: *A performance at the Royal Palace.*

🖳 www.majorcineplex.com ⊠ 7/F, Central World Plaza, ☎ 025 155 555, 🚇 Chit Lom; or ⊠ 7/F, MBK Centre, corner of Thanon Phayathai and Thanon Rama I, ☎ 026 116 444, 🚇 National Stadium. **SF Cinema City**, ⊠ 6/F, Emporium Shopping Centre, Soi 24, Sukhumvit Rd, ☎ 022 609 333, 🚇 Phrom Phong. **Apex Cinemas**, 🖳 www.apexsiam-square.com 🚇 Siam for all Apex cinemas. **Lido Multiplex**, ⊠ 256 Thanon Rama I, Siam Square, ☎ 022 526 498. **Scala**, ⊠ Siam Square, Soi 1, ☎ 022 512 861. **Siam**, ⊠ 352 Rama I Road, Siam Square, ☎ 022 513 508.

Theatre

Traditional Thai art forms, both dance and theatre, are performed at a small number of theatres in Bangkok. A visit to the puppet theatre can be combined with eating and shopping at the **Suan Lum Night Bazaar** (*see* page 50) while the **Ruen Thep** Thai **dance shows** offer the option of an evening buffet meal before performances. The dance shows at the Oriental are a combined dinner-and-performance set.

Joe Louis Puppet Theatre

Puppet theatre is a traditional Thai art form that was in danger of dying out until rescued by a man, **Sakorn Yangkeowsod**, who was nicknamed Joe Louis. The shows enact adventures from the *Ramakien* and are enjoyable for adults as well as children, and there is an accompanying English-language talk-over that explains the plot. ⌧ Suan Lum Night Bazaar, Rama IV Rd, ☎ 022 529 683, ⌨ www.joelouistheatre.com ⏲ 19:30; Sat–Sun 17:00, ⛴ Siam

Patravadi Theatre

This theatre is located in Thonburi, on the west side of the Chao Phraya River, but it is worth the journey if there is something on that catches your interest. Consult their website for details of current performances. ⌧ Soi Wat Rakang, Thonburi, ☎ 024 127 287, ⌨ www.patravadi theatre.com ⏲ 19:00, ⛴ Wat Rakhang or Wang Lang Pier.

Ruen Thep

Classical Thai dance in the setting of the Silom Village complex. There is a touristy feel to the whole show but the dances are authentic. ⌧ Silom Village, 286 Silom Rd, ☎ 026 357 521 ⌨ www.silom

Below: *Classical Thai dances are slow and stately, enlivened by brilliant costumes and precise movements.*

Right: *Thai Boxing is becoming increasingly popular with visitors and there are two stadiums in Bangkok.*

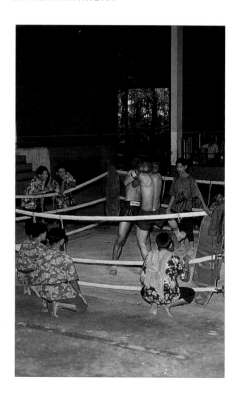

Thai Boxing

Thai boxing, *muay Thai*, is now well known outside Thailand and there are two stadiums in Bangkok where regular bouts take place. Tickets need not be booked in advance but you should arrive outside the stadium a good half-hour before the start time to secure a seat. The most expensive seats are close to the front of the ring but many visitors prefer not to be too close to the action and enjoy watching from further back.

Lumphini Stadium
⊠ Rama IV Rd
☎ 022 528 765
⊕ Mon, Wed–Thu 18:00; Sun 17:00
💰 B220–B1000

Ratchadamnoen Boxing Stadium
⊠ 1 Ratchadamnoen Noi
☎ 022 814 205
⊕ Tue, Fri 18:30–23:00, Sat 17:00, 20:00
💰 B220–B1000

village.co.th ⊕ 20:30–21:20; dinner 19:00–21:20, 🚣 Central Pier or Oriental Pier, 🚇 Surasak

Sala Rim Naam
Classical Thai dance in a classy setting on the other side of the river to the Oriental Hotel itself; boat transport is provided. Despite being rather expensive, these shows are often full and reservations are recommended. The food is mediocre but the dances are absorbing. ⊠ The Oriental Hotel, 48 Oriental Avenue, ☎ 024 372 918 ext. 3344, 🖥 www.mandarinoriental.com, ⊕ 19:00, 💰 B1850, 🚣 The Oriental Pier, 🚇 Saphan Taksin

Nightclubs

Bed Supperclub

One of the most chic places to see and be seen in, Bed Supperclub has queues forming nightly and if you want to secure one of the all-white beds to lounge on, a reservation is essential. Food is optional but it helps maintain the air of classy decadence that draws in the punters. Various mini-shows, often featuring fashion themes, provide entertainment and there is an adjoining bar with loud music.
✉ 26 Sukhumvit Soi 11, ☎ 026 513 537, 🖥 www.bedsupperclub.com 🚇 Nana, ⏰ 19:30–01:00 nightly, 💰 Tue, Fri–Sat B500, including 2 drinks, Sun–Mon, Wed–Thu B400; dinner B1090
Remember! Photo ID is required at the door.

Brown Sugar

A well-established and reliably good jazz joint which also serves decent food. One of the best all-round places for a night's gentle relaxation with music.
✉ 231/2 Soi Sarasin, ☎ 022 501 826, 🚇 Ratchadamri, M Silom, ⏰ Fri–Sun 17:00–02:00, Mon–Thu 11:00–14:00, 17:00–01:00; live music Sun–Mon 22:00–01:00, Tue–Thu 20:45–01:00, Fri–Sat 19:45–01:00.

Concept CM^2

A popular nightclub that has been around for ten years and it still draws in a healthy crowd of party people. There is an Italian-style restaurant so a whole night can be made of a visit here. Big bands play regularly and there is also the **Boom Room** where DJs spin faster sounds.
✉ Basement, Novotel Hotel, 29 Soi 38, Sukhumvit Rd, ☎ 027 136 048 🖥 www.cm2bkk.com 🚇 Siam, ⏰ daily 21:00–02:00; ladies night Mon (free admission) 💰 Sun–Thu B200, Fri–Sat B550; price includes B150 discount on first drink.

Mojos

People who know say Mojos has the best sound system of any Bangkok nightspot. The retro décor is 1950s style and the blues music suits this perfectly. American food like spare ribs and burgers are on tap, though Thai food is also available, and the cocktails are all fairly priced around B150.
✉ 10/20 Soi 33, Sukhumvit Rd ☎ 022 608 429, 🖥 www.bangkokmojos.com ⏰ 16:00–02:00, daily, 🚇 Asok, M Sukhumvit

Mystique

Another one of the super-cool clubs that Bangkok is famous for, complete with funky wall hangings and a sea water tank where snappy little sharks glide around bored almost to death. Big-name DJs often appear but there is also a chill-out area on the rooftop. The last Monday of every month is the big disco night and the cover charge increases.

✉ 71/8 Soi 31, Sukhumvit Rd
☎ 023 622 374
🖥 www.mystique.com
🕓 Tue–Sat 20:00–14:00
🚇 Asok,
Ⓜ Sukhumvit
💰 *Thu B550, Fri–Sat B650, including two drinks.*

Q Bar

Despite the dark interior and black hue, all is not doom and gloom at the Q Bar. You can boogie downstairs or chat and cool down upstairs. The list of cocktails is spectacular and the music gets wicked when top-drawer DJs take control.

✉ 34 Soi 11, Sukhumvit Rd

☎ 022 523 274
🖥 www.qbarbangkok.com
🕓 20:00–01:00 daily,
💰 *Mon–Thu B400, Fri–Sun B600, includes two free drinks,*
🚇 Nana

Xcentrix

Four floors for your enjoyment, starting with a trendy bar on the first level enhanced by its aquatic 'lava wall'. Bring your dancing shoes for the house music upstairs or carry on to the third level for a modernist, space-age area. The rooftop level should offer some respite from the noise and people.

✉ 14/5 Soi 4, Silom Rd,
☎ 026 329 669,
💰 *Tue–Sun 18:00–04:00,*
🚇 Sala Daeng

Bars with Music
The Club

The décor is a little different from the usual Bangkok ingredients, aiming to conjure up a

Mediterranean feel with a whitewashed wall on which fishing boats hang. DJ-driven music from early evening and food on the menu alongside jugs of Singha for B200.

✉ Khao San Rd,
☎ 026 291 010,
🕓 23:00–01:00 daily,
🚆 Tha Athit

Hidden Hipness

The name suggests this place is hard to find and you will need to look carefully, and pass many a more alluring and glitzy bar, to find the **'HIP'** sign signifying this neat little joint. Come here for a relaxed drink and to escape the more frenzied scene out on the street. DJs spin music from around 21:00.

✉ Soi 4, Silom Rd,
☎ 0 1612 7093,
🕓 19:00–01:00 daily,
🚆 Sala Daeng

Radio City

There are some places to hang out in Patpong and keep

your self-respect, and Radio City is definitely one such venue. Live bands play straight-forward rock and the Elvis impersonator is reason enough to pay a visit.

✉ 76/1–3 Patpong 1,
☎ 022 664 567,
🕐 18:00–02:00 daily,
🚇 Sala Daeng

Re-Wind

As the name indicates, Re-Wind is a trip back in time – to the 1970s and '80s. The music gets going around 22:00 with either a DJ or a band. The style is informal and easy-going.

✉ 2/F, Camp Davis, 88 Soi 24, Sukhumvit Rd
☎ 026 603 842,
🕐 19:00–01:00, daily,
🚇 Phrom Phong

Saxophone

A pub and restaurant with live jazz and blues every night of the week. Saxophone has been around for a number of years and knows its stuff.

✉ 3/8 Phayathai Rd,

Victory Monument, Thanon Phrayathai,
☎ 022 465 472,
💻 www.saxophone bar.com
🕐 20:00–01:00 daily,
Ⓜ Victory Monument

Zuk Bar

A stylish hotel with an ultra-stylish and very cool bar, decorated with classic Thai artefacts and benefiting from an unhurried atmosphere. Posh sofas to recline on and classy music from professional DJs.

✉ Ground Level, Sukhothai Hotel, South Sathon Rd,
☎ 023 448 888,
🕐 Mon–Thu 15:00–01:00; Fri–Sun 13:00–01:00,
🚇 Sala Daeng
Ⓜ Lumphini

Sunset Street

One of the more pleasant places on Khao San Road for a drink and some atmosphere. Of the three bars, **Sabai** has the most cozy character. The **Sunset Bar** itself has live music while **Sanook** is a more hip-hop fun kind of place.

✉ 199 Khao San Rd,
☎ 0228 225 565,
💻 www.sunset street.com
🕐 Sabai Bar 20:00–01:00; Sanook Bar 18:00–01:00; Sunset Bar 20:00–01:00
🚢 Tha Athit

Below: *There are hundreds of bars and clubs to choose from and they range from the highly sophisticated to the downright raunchy.*

EXCURSIONS
Ayutthaya

Ayutthaya was the capital of Siam, as Thailand was then called, from 1350 until it was attacked and destroyed by Burmese forces in 1767. It was as a result of this attack that a new capital was established further down the Chao Phraya River at Bangkok, then a mere fishing village. The ruins of ancient Ayutthaya have made it a **World Heritage site** and the remains of the various temples are what visitors come to see.

The tourist office is opposite the Chao Sam Phraya National Museum, on Si Sanphet Rd, ☎ 035 246 076, open daily from 08:30 to 16:30. Both the museum (Wed–Sun, 09:00–16:00) and the tourist office are worth a visit and the free map will help you find your way around the temples. Bikes can be hired and are a useful way of getting about because the temples are spread around and too far apart to walk. *Samlors* and *tuk-tuks* are readily available.

Below: *The temple ruins at Ayutthaya.*

On a day trip, or even with an overnight stay, there are too many temple ruins to visit and some of them are only of interest to archaeologists. The ones to see include **Wat Phra Mahathat**, complete with the photogenic *bodhi* tree growing around a Buddha head. **Wat Phra Si Sanphet** is worth admiring for its *chedi* containing the ruins of long-forgotten kings, and **Viharn Monkol Bopit** is home to a huge bronze Buddha, which is over 12 metres high.

Getting There & Away

Early fast **trains** to Ayutthaya from Bangkok's Hua Lampong station depart at 07:00, 08:00 and 09:05, then 11:35 and 14:30. The journey time is one hour and 40 minutes. From Ayutthaya station, follow the crowds to the ferry pier a hundred metres away and take the short journey across the river; from the other side it is a five-minute walk to the town centre.

Above: *Take a train over the River Kwai, out of the capital.*

Daily **buses** from the Northern Bus Terminal take as long as the trains so the train is more convenient. All Bangkok travel agents offer package trips to Ayutthaya, some making one leg of the journey by boat.

Kanchanaburi

Kanchanaburi is a town east of Bangkok where the infamous Bridge on the River Kwai was constructed during World War II. The first bridge was built of wood, replaced by a steel one within months, by forced labour under the Japanese in 1943. The bridge was part of the plan to construct a railway line to Burma through 420km (261 miles) of mountainous terrain and some 300,000 Asians were persuaded to work on the railway, having no idea of the awful conditions and starvation diet they would be subjected to. In addition, 60,000 prisoners of war – Australian, British and Dutch mostly – were brought to Kanchanaburi to join the work teams. One in three Asians died, although the plight of the prisoners of war, with a death rate of 20%, has received more attention.

Sleeping and Eating (Kanchanaburi)
River Kwai Hotel,
✉ Saeng Chuto Rd,
☎ 034 513 348,
🖳 www.riverkwai.com
Not by the river but the best hotel in town and a swimming pool. On the road between the railway station and tourist office.
Jolly Frog Backpackers, ✉ 28 Soi China, off Maenam Kwai Rd and by the river. ☎ 034 514 579, 🖳 www.jollyfrog.fsnet.co.uk A range of rooms, including air-con huts with private bathrooms. Attractive location.
Sabaijit Restaurant,
✉ Saeng Chuto Rd. Just past the River Kwai Hotel, inexpensive but hygienic and with a large menu in English. The Appache bar on the other side of the street is good for live music at night.

The town itself has charm, has a good visitor infrastructure and it is easy to get about; *samlors* and *tuk-tuks* cost about B50 for short trips from, say, the railway station to the tourist office. The tourist office, ☎ 0-3451-1200, is open daily from 08:30 to 16:30. A Tourist Police post, ☎ 0-3451-2795, operates from here as well.

From the main Kanchanaburi railway station, you can walk north for the bridge (about 2 km/1.3 miles) or south (3km) for the tourist office. The bus station for first-class buses from Bangkok is just north of the tourist office, a two-minute walk away. You can collect a town map at the tourist office and wander off to find many places to eat and a wide choice of accommodation for the night.

It is possible to visit Kanchanaburi by using the two-hour, first-class bus service and return to Bangkok the same day. But the range of attractive, river-side guesthouses makes an overnight stay well worth considering. On the road between the main railway station and the tourist office, Saeng Chuto Rd, there are some hotels and restaurants but it is worth staying closer to the river along Maenam Kwai Rd. This is the main visitor area and here you will find an abundance of guesthouses, places to eat, bike hire, internet joints and bars.

The Bridge and Museums

The **Bridge on the River Kwai** that you see today was rebuilt after the war, using parts of the completed steel bridge that was bombed by the Allies shortly after its completion. If arriving by train, you can go straight to the bridge by staying on the

Getting There & Away (Kanchanaburi)

Train: The best way to reach Kanchanaburi, though not the fastest, is a scenic train ride from Thonburi station in Bangkok. Note: this is not the main Hua Lampong station but a smaller one on the other side of the river. Trains depart daily at 07:45 and 13:50 and take nearly three hours. Seats cannot be booked in advance so give yourself enough time to reach the station and purchase your ticket. On Saturday, Sunday and public holidays there is a special train at 06:30 from Bangkok's Hua Lampong station. This train can be booked in advance.

Bus: Buses depart from Bangkok's Southern Bus Terminal; be sure to get a first-class bus, departing every 15 minutes, or it will take forever.

Minibus: Travel agents, especially in Khao San Rd, run a variety of tours to Kanchanaburi and they save you from having to get to the Southern Bus Terminal or the Thonburi railway station. Best of all is a straightforward minibus service to and from Kanchanaburi.

Left: *Afternoon tea at the old Railway Hotel, now the Sofitel Central, in Hua Hin.*

train for River Kwai Bridge station, the one after the main Kanchanaburi station.

The town of Kanchanaburi has several museums. The **Thailand-Burma Railway Centre** is easy to find, being just across the road from the train station. If you only visit one museum in Kanchanaburi, be sure to make it this one. It is open daily from 09:00 to 17:00 and entry costs B60.

JEATH is an acronym of six of the countries involved in the railway: Japan, England, Australia, America, Thailand and Holland. The **JEATH War Museum** is now showing its age but remains a heartfelt homage to those who died. It is situated 5km from the bridge, less than a 1km from the tourist office, at the southern end of town. Open daily from 08:30 to 18:00 (B30).

To visit the **World War II Museum**, just follow the signs from the bridge but if your time is limited then give it a miss because it is the least interesting of the three museums. Open daily from 08:00 to 18:00 (B30)

<u>Sleeping and Eating (Kanchanaburi)</u>
River Kwai Hotel, ✉ Saeng Chuto Rd, ☎ 034 513348, 💻 www.riverkwai.com Not by the river but the best hotel in town and a swimming pool. On the road between the railway station and tourist office.
Jolly Frog Backpackers, ✉ 28 Soi China, off Maenam Kwai Rd and by the river. ☎ 0-34 514579, 💻 www.jollyfrog. fsnet.co.uk A range of rooms, including air-con huts with private bathrooms. Attractive location.
Sabaijit Restaurant, ✉ Saeng Chuto Rd. Just past the River Kwai Hotel, inexpensive but hygienic and with a large menu in English. The Appache bar on the other side of the street is good for live music at night.

Hua Hin

Hua Hin is situated to the south of Bangkok, taking over three hours by train but faster by bus from Bangkok. An overnight stay is really necessary to make a visit worthwhile as this would give time for a lazy lounge on the beach and for enjoyment of the town's nightlife.

Each June there is a **jazz festival** (🖳 www.huahinjazzfestival.com). Hua Hin went on the map because Thai royalty chose it as a getaway and built a palace here (not open to the public) and then in the 1920s the Bangkok-Malaysia railway line passed by and a station was opened. This led to the building of the classic Railway Hotel (now a five-star Sofitel hotel) and well-heeled travellers followed in its wake. Even if not staying at the Sofitel Hotel, it is worth seeing the colonial-style, open-air lobby and **topiary gardens**, although the place is a little too manicured for its own good and bedrooms are pricey.

The tourist information office is on the corner of Damnern Kasem and Rd and Phetkasem, ☎ 032 532433, and opens daily between 08:30 and 16:30 (although between April and November it may only open on weekdays). A few doors down is the main post office with internet access upstairs. Hua Hin is small enough to get around on foot and there are plenty of shops catering to visitors.Hua Hin has become more popular than ever with visitors and booking accommodation in advance can be fairly essential during high season. Despite the crowds, Hua Hin is a low-key beach resort compared to what you may find in others parts of the country. The best part of the five-kilometre beach is in front of and to the south of the Sofitel hotel and there are bars and restaurants close to the sand. To the north of the hotel, the beach itself is less inviting but there are pleasant restaurants perched at the end of small piers that jut out into the sea.

Getting There & Away

The first **train** to Hua Hin from Bangkok's Hua Lampong station departs at 07:45, arriving in Hua Hin at 11:00, and the second train departs at 13:00 and arrives at 16:40. Delays are not uncommon and a bus is a better bet.

Daily **buses** from the Southern Bus Terminal take about an hour and a half.

Festivals

Mid-January and late February: **The Chinese New Year**, celebrated with gusto by the Thai–Chinese. Be in Chinatown for lion dancers, lots of fireworks and street parades. Late February to mid-April: **The kite-flying season** and Sanam Luang or Lumphini Park is the place to be. Mid-April: S**ongkhran**, the most celebratory of Thailand's national holidays and, for the visitor, a time when you can expect to be doused with water on the street.

Below: *An aerial view of Hua Hin.*

Above: *Traffic in Bangkok builds up during the rush hours and, especially during heavy rainfall, comes almost to a halt.*

Using Chao Phraya Express Boats
Useful stops include:
Central Pier also called Sathorn, connects with a Skytrain station (Saphan Taksin)
Oriental (N1) for Silom Rd
Tha Rachawongse (N5) also called Rajawong, for Chinatown
Tha Thien (N8) for Wat Pho and cross-river ferry to Wat Arun
Tha Chang for the Grand Palace
Bangkok Noi (N11) for the railway station serving Kanchanaburi
Tha Phra Athit (N13) for Khao San Rd.

Tourist Information

Any journey in Bangkok can take up time so it makes sense to call in at the tourist information office at the airport and collect maps and general information about tours and travel advice for any excursions you might be planning. You can also check with the tourist office as to which bus to catch from the airport for your hotel.

In the city, the Bangkok Information Centre, ☎ 022 257 612, ☺ daily from 09:00 to 19:00, located by Phra Pinklao Bridge on Phra Athit Rd in Banglamphu. If coming by boat, turn left after exiting from Phra Athit pier (N13) and go down the road a short way.

The Tourism Authority of Thailand (TAT), 🖳 www.tat.or.th have an office also in Banglamphu on Rajdamnoen Nok, ☎ 022 829 773, ☺ daily 08:30–16:30. Their headquarters are awkward to reach at ✉ 1600 Phetchaburi Mai Rd, near Soi 21 off Sukhumvit Rd, and it is easier to telephone if you have an enquiry, ☎ 022 505 500.

Thailand Tourist Offices Abroad: **United Kingdom:** ✉ 3rd Floor, Brook House, 98–99 Jermyn St, London SWIY 6EE, ☎ 020 7925 2511, 🖳 www.thaismile.co.uk **USA:** 61 Broadway, Suite 2810, New York, NY 10006, ☎ 212 432 0433, ✆ info@tatny.com

Entry Requirements

Most nationalities can enter Thailand without a visa for 30 days and your passport will be stamped for this length of time upon arrival. Make sure your passport is valid for six months from the time of your arrival. A 60-day visa can be applied for in advance through the Thai embassy in your home country. Within Thailand, visa extensions can be arranged at an immigration office but there will be a charge for this service. There is a departure tax of B500.

The Immigration Office in Bangkok is on ⊠ Soi Suan Phlu, off South Sathorn Rd, ☎ 022 873 101, ⏰ Mon–Fri, 08:30–16:30; Sat 08:30–midday. Embassies and Consulates, 🖵 www.thaiembassy.org

United Kingdom:
⊠ 29-30 Queens Gate, London SW7 5JB, ☎ 020 7589 2944.
USA: ⊠ 1024 Wisconsin Ave NW, Washington DC 20007, ☎ 202 944 3600.

Customs

Visitors to Thailand are allowed to bring in one litre of spirits or wine and 200 cigarettes (or 250g of tobacco). On leaving the country – remember there is a departure tax of B500, payable in cash at the airport – you need a licence from the Office of Archaeology and National Museums if you are exporting an antique or religious image. In theory, this includes figures of the Buddha but the rule is only applied to genuinely old such figures. Any reputable shop selling antiques should be able to arrange for such a licence on your behalf.

Health Requirements

There are no essential inoculation requirements for entry into Thailand but *see* the Health Precautions section on page 90.

Getting There by Air

The highest fares will be in high season, between mid-Nov and mid-Feb and during the European summer months of Jul and Aug. From the United Kingdom there are frequent non-stop flights from London and Manchester to Bangkok, with a flight time of around 12 hours. Less expensive flights usually involve a stopover, often somewhere in the Middle East, and may be inconvenient and add considerable time to the journey. An exception is Austrian Airlines because the stopover in Vienna is a very short one. Expect to pay around £500 for a non-stop flight.

Major airlines flying to Bangkok from London and Europe include:
Air France 🖵 www.airfrance.com
Austrian Airlines 🖵 www.austrianairlines.com
British Airways 🖵 www.ba.com
Emirates 🖵 www.emirates.com
EVA Airways 🖵 www.evaair.com
KLM 🖵 www.klm.com
Lufthansa 🖵 www.lufthansa.com
Malaysia Airlines 🖵 www.malaysia-airlines.com
Quantas 🖵 www.quantas.co.uk
Singapore Airlines 🖵 www.singaporeair.com
Thai Airways 🖵 www.thaiair.com
Turkish Airlines 🖵 www.thy.com
From the east or west coast of the USA and

Canada flight time is around 20 hours and nearly always involves a stopover, although Thai Airways do run a direct flight from New York. In high season, expect to pay around $1000 for a flight from the west coast and up to $200 more from the east coast.

Major airlines flying to Bangkok from the USA and Canada include:

Air Canada 🖳 www.aircanada.com

Cathay Pacific 🖳 www.cathaypacific.com

China Airlines 🖳 www.china-airlines.com

Delta 🖳 www.delta.com

Lufthansa 🖳 www.lufthansa.com

Thai Airways 🖳 www.thaiair.com

United Airlines 🖳 www.united.com

Bangkok's New Airport

Bangkok's Don Muang international airport is scheduled to give way to the new Suvarnabhumi Airport in late 2006 and, after a number of postpone-ments, this date now looks fairly certain. Suvarnabhumi Airport is 30km east of Bangkok and its one large terminal will han-dle international and domestic flights.

A bus service from the airport into the city centre will be operat-ing, along the same lines as the existing service from Don Muang. Staff at the ticket counter for the airport bus will advise as to what route best suits your hotel loca-tion and, in most cases, the bus will stop con-veniently close to your accommodation. A taxi from the new airport will cost around B300 and there will be a coupon system in oper-ation. Ignore the touts who may pester you politely in the arrivals hall. A train service connecting the airport with the city centre is not yet completed.

What to Pack

Take as little as possible with you because, unless shopping is simply not on your agenda, you will need maximum luggage space for all the things you will be buying when you get there. Anything you plan to purchase for your trip – clothes, non-prescrip-tion medicines, shoes, spectacles, luggage – is going to cost less in Bangkok. Many visitors bring too many clothes for the hot climate and you can get by with light cotton gar-ments most of the time. Books are expen-sive in Bangkok so bring all your reading material with you.

Money Matters

Currency: The unit of currency is the baht (B), divided into 100 satang. Banknotes come in B10, B50, B100, B500 and B1000, and increase in size as their value goes up. Coins come in B1, B5 and B10 and there are also 25- and 50-satang coins.

Exchange: There is no black market in the Thai baht and money can be exchanged in banks or at the numerous exchange booths dotted around the city. Banks open Mon–Fri, 08:30 to either 15:30 or 16:30 and exchange booths in areas like Sukhumvit stay open a lot longer. Hotels will change money at any time but the exchange rate will be lower than any bank or exchange booth.

Cheques and Cards: Traveller's cheques in sterling, dollar and euro are accepted at banks and exchange booths as well as some hotels. Credit cards are accepted in many shops, restaurants and hotels. Using your bank card you should be able to withdraw Thai baht from ATMs, readily available throughout the city and open 24 hours. Keep traveller's cheques separate from bank cards and always keep separate your list of traveller's cheque numbers and the contact telephone numbers for lost cheques

and bank cards. Keeping a list of these numbers in cyberspace using your e-mail account is a good idea.

Bargaining: Bargaining is common in Bangkok and not just in obvious places like markets and street stalls. Fixed prices apply in department stores and most shops in the shopping malls but, as a general rule, where prices are not displayed on merchandise you can expect some polite negotiation to result in a reduction of anything from 10% to 50%.

City Transport

Bangkok is vast and sprawling in size and getting from A to B can be a prolonged and frustrating experience so it helps a lot to plan journeys.

The **BTS Skytrain** (🖥 www.bts.co.th) is the most convenient way of getting around the city, although it doesn't go everywhere and sometimes needs to be used in conjunc-

---

Hospitals in Bangkok
Bangkok General Hospital, ✉ 2 Soi Soonvija 7, Phetchaburi Mai Rd, ☎ 023 103 000; emergency ☎ 023 103 456; 24-hour call centre ☎ 023 103 344, 🖥 www. bangkokhospital.com This hospital also has a dental surgery.
Travmin Bangkok Medical Centre, ✉ 8th Floor, Alma Link Building, 25 Soi Chitlom, Ploenchit Rd, ☎ 026 551 024
Bumrungrad Hospital, ✉ 33 Soi 3, Sukhumvit Rd, ☎ 026 671 00; emergency ☎ 026 672 999; 🖥 www. bumrungrad.com

tion with a river boat, taxi or metro. There are two Skytrain lines: one runs from Mo Chit in the north, near Chatuchak Weekend Market, to the east of the city along Sukhumvit Rd. The other line runs from the bottom end of Silom Rd near the river to National Stadium in the west of the city. The two lines intersect at Siam station and trains run from 06:00 to midnight. Stored tickets can be purchased at the stations and, apart from saving a little money, they save the time queuing up to buy tickets from a machine for each and every trip. A three day/four night Tourist Pass is B280 and covers four days if purchased in the morning – while 30-day passes cover any 10 trips for B250, 15 trips for B300 and 30 trips for B540.

The **MRT metro** (🖳 www.mrta.co.th) runs from 05:00 to midnight and the line connects Hua Lampong railway station with the north of the city. Skytrain's Sala Daeng station connects with Silom metro station and a short walk connects Skytrain's Asok station with the metro's Sukhumvit station. Tickets are bought from machines at the stations.

The **Chao Phraya Express Boat** service is very useful for getting across the city and boats run from 06:00 to around 19:00. Fares are B8–15 and tickets are bought onboard from a conductor. If the boat is not carrying a flag then it stops at every pier but some boats (06:00–09:00 and midday to 19:00) carry either a yellow or orange flag, indicating a limited number of stops at only the main piers. Information panels at the main piers explain the different flagged services.
Taxis are metered and air-conditioned, though you may find that with a sudden downpour of rain – when everyone wants a taxi – you will have to negotiate a (higher) price for your destination. Fares start at B35 for the first 2km and are generally good value, adding B4.50 per km for 2–12 km and B5 per km for 13–20km. There is a congestion charge when the taxi moves no faster than 6km per hour, adding B1.25 per minute.

Tuk-tuks are the three-wheeled buggies with open sides that you see everywhere in Bangkok. They can be a fast way of getting somewhere because of their seemingly reckless skill in weaving in and out of traffic. The downside is your exposure to dense traffic fumes, non-English-speaking drivers most of the time and the hassle of having to negotiate a fare for every journey. It helps to be able to name a big hotel, major attraction or one of the bigger shopping malls. The average fare for a short hop is B50.

Canal boats operate like the Chao Phraya Express and stop at designated piers and although they are not as comfortable they do open a non-touristy window on Bangkok life. The most useful route links the Banglamphu area, at Tha Phanta, with Sukhumvit Rd at Tha Asok.

Business Hours

Most shops open seven days a week from 08:00/09:30 to between 18:00 and 21:00, though some shops may close on Sun. Offices, including government ones, usually open Mon–Fri from 08:30 to 16:30. Banks open on weekdays from 08:30 to either 15:30 or 16:30.

Time Difference

Time in Thailand is 7 hours ahead of GMT and 6 hours ahead of British Summer Time. It is twelve hours ahead of US Eastern Time.

Communications

Internet access is available across the city at a variety of Internet-dedicated shops and in areas like Sukhumvit Rd and Khao San Rd such places will stay open until late at night. Most hotels will have Internet use for guests, although the rate charged will usually be higher than on the street. Public **phone boxes** are readily available and for local calls phone cards are available in units of B50, B100, B200 and B250; coins can also be used. International calls can be made using Thaicards, phone cards issued by CAT (Communications Authority of Thailand) and available from post offices and shops like 7-Eleven. There are also phone cards issued by private companies and used in their own

International dialling codes

If dialling from abroad, Thailand's international code is 66, followed by the Bangkok number but leaving off the initial zero. For international directory enquiries in Bangkok, call 100.

UK	44
US	1
Australia	61
Canada	1

phone booths; Lenso is the biggest company and their cards are available from 7-Eleven and the like. Phone booths for international calls are all over the city. Check with your **mobile phone** provider as to the use of your phone in Bangkok; most can be used, although you should confirm the current rates for receiving and making telephone calls and/ or texting. Bangkok's main **post office** is on Thanon Charoen Krung (New Road) which runs from the bottom of Silom Rd. It is open 24 hours and has the advantage of offering some peace and quiet when making phone calls or using the Internet access that is also provided.

Electricity

Electricity is 220 volts AC. You may need some travel-plug adaptors if packing your own electrical equipment as the usual type of plug uses two round pins, though sometimes the pins are of the flat-blade type. *See* 🖳 www.kropla.com

Weights and Measures

Thailand uses the metric system for weights and measures. To convert pounds to kilograms, multiply by 0.45 (by 2.21 for the reverse); inches to centimetres, multiply by 2.54 (0.39 for the reverse), yards to metres by 0.91 (1.09 for the reverse).

Health Precautions

It is advisable that visitors are protected against hepatitis A, polio and typhoid. Malaria is transmitted by mosquito bites but this is very unlikely to happen in Bangkok and you do not need to take any preventive medicine. Rabies, too, is rare in the city but keep away from stray dogs just to be sure. Non-prescriptive medicines, and some only available on prescription in your home country, are readily available from pharmacies and advice can be sought from professionally trained, English-speaking pharmacists. It is highly recommended that you take out travel insurance in your home country for the duration of your stay in Thailand. This should include health cover and theft or loss of property and money. In the unlikely event of having to make a claim, you will need some documentation: a hospital bill for medical care or a police report for theft.

Health Services

Private health and dental clinics, and good hospitals, are not hard to find in Bangkok. Standards are high and the clinics and hospitals are staffed by English-speaking professionals.

Personal Safety

Common sense will see you safely through a visit to Bangkok. There are pickpockets in crowded sights and on buses but it would be foolish anywhere to expose your wallet or purse in a way that would tempt a thief. Many hotels have lockers in the bedrooms or a central locker for the safe-keeping of valuables. Keep a photocopy of your passport, travel and insurance documents and emergency telephone numbers for bank card loss separate from the originals; consider scanning them and keeping them as a file in your e-mail account. Scams are not uncommon, especially around sights like the Grand Palace and Jim Thompson's House, and usually consist of trying to persuade you that the sight is temporarily closed and to take an inexpensive tour or taxi with them to somewhere else. You won't get mugged but you will be taken to shops where the scam merchant receives a commission and your time will be wasted. Beware of anyone offering anything that seems too good a deal to resist.

Emergencies

In an emergency, telephone the English-speaking tourist police on ☎ 1155 (24 hours). They will advise you on what to do as regards a medical emergency requiring an ambulance or the police or the fire service. Telephoning 1155 is better than phoning the police direct (☎ 191) or the fire service (☎ 199).

Etiquette

Thai culture forbids any criticism of royalty and visitors should bear this in mind. Related to this sense of respect, there is a strict dress code when visiting the Grand Palace or other sights associated with Thai royalty. Thais do not respect acts of overt aggression, verbal or otherwise, and a loud-mouthed Westerner getting angry about some lapse in service only invites ridicule. Shaking hands upon meeting someone is readily understood but not as prevalent as in the West and a more common gesture is the placing of the hands together under the chin, known as a wai.

Language

English is widely understood and spoken in Bangkok in places where visitors are likely to eat, drink or shop and if you do encounter a situation where English is not understood there is usually someone in the vicinity who can help interpret. A few words of Thai, though, go a long way and the usual polite salutation in place of good morning/afternoon is *sawat-dii-khrap* (to a man) or *sawat-dii-kha* (to a woman). Thank you is *khawp khun*.

INDEX OF SIGHTS

GENERAL INDEX

GENERAL INDEX

General Index

GENERAL INDEX